COMPE**   **ONS

Questions   pics

AN EN

Eric H. Koth and Tom Aberson

Compelling Conversations:
Questions and Quotations on Timeless Topics
An Engaging ESL Textbook for Advanced Students
Copyright © 2006, Eric H. Roth and Toni W. Aberson
Copyright © 2008, Second Edition
ISBN: 1-4196-5828-X
Library of Congress Reg. # TX 6-377-924

Printed by CreateSpace
To order additional copies, share comments,
ask questions, or contribute quotations
please visit www.compellingconversations.com

Cover photo from iStock.com/Cosmonaut Creative Media LLC
All other photos by Laurie Selik

Chimayo Press

**Dedicated to
Dani Herbert Joseph Roth**
(1937–1997)

A global citizen, he could talk with almost
anyone, in six different languages, and share a
laugh. This book attempts to capture some of
his generous spirit, wit, and curiosity.

"Own only what you can always carry with
you: know languages, know countries, know
people. Let your memory be your travel bag."
Alexander Solzhenitsyn (1918–),
Russian writer and historian

ACKNOWLEDGEMENTS

Laurie Selik
Zigmund Vays
Jim Valentine
Idalia Rodriguez
George Rodriguez
Adam Rado
Regina Pablo
Sharon Myers
Nina Ito
Alla Kogan
Oleg Khalkevich
Paula Johnson
Ben Hammer
Marina Goldshteyn
Ronit Frazam
Rosa Dreizin
Mark Chumley
Elaine Afable
Lucienne Aarsen

Several people helped in the development, research, and creation of this hybrid ESL textbook. Several ESL professionals and students have offered numerous suggestions at critical moments in developing this conversation book. Here is a brief, and no means complete, list of kind individuals who have helped improve this book.

"Everybody is a student, and everybody is a teacher" goes the saying. This book reflects that philosophy. The eager students that worked with us during the last decade in various ESL classrooms have expanded our world.

From the adult students at the Santa Monica Adult Education Center, Indianapolis Ivy Tech, and Community Enhancement Services attending classes while working difficult jobs to energetic American Language Institute students in Long Beach, Santa Monica Community College, and UCLA Extension, you have shared your experiences and insights. Thank you.

Naturally, we also owe an exceptional debt to the ambitious USC graduate students at the American Language Institute; we have often shared questions, proverbs, and laughs. Your enthusiasm pushed us to complete this project. Our lively conversations, in and out of the classroom, have exceeded expectations and created small classroom communities where we could take chances and develop our skills. The adoption of this book by the Conversation Club promises to lead to even more compelling conversations.

Please visit our website, www.compellingconversations.com, to offer feedback, suggest additional topics, or contribute questions or quotations for future editions.

We hope this rich collection of questions, proverbs, and quotations will spark many compelling conversations. Let's keep talking, sharing, and learning together!

Eric H. Roth
Toni Aberson

"Gratitude is the memory of the heart."

French proverb

"No one is as capable of gratitude as one who has emerged from the kingdom of the night."

Elie Wiesel (1928–), American writer and Nobel Peace Prize winner

INTRODUCTION

The art of conversation, once considered the sign of a civilized individual, seems less common today. Yet I treasure the moments of sharing experiences, collecting news, and exchanging ideas. I make a point of knowing my neighbors, allowing casual greetings to become long conversations, and making time to explore in depth the feelings and perceptions of friends and relatives. These natural conversations provide information, encouragement, laughs, and pleasure.

Many people say that they are too busy to have long talks. Other people prefer to watch television, play computer games, or listen to the radio rather than talk to relatives and friends. Sometimes people feel too shy to speak to the people next to them. Many Americans have forgotten how to hold good, deep conversations, or even a friendly chat on the phone. I suspect this lack of real communication lessens their daily joy.

Of course, people learning English as a second, third, or fourth language face even more barriers to a satisfying conversation in English. First, English remains a confusing, difficult, and strange language. It's easy to feel uncomfortable when speaking in this new tongue. What questions do I ask? How can I keep a conversation going? What vocabulary words are needed? How do I show agreement, or disagreement, in a lively, yet polite way? How can I share my experiences in a clear manner? How can I have better, more engaging conversations in English?

Compelling Conversations: Questions and Quotations on Timeless Topics addresses these issues for both native and non-native speakers. The focus is on learning by doing, and making good mistakes. (Good mistakes, by the way, are natural mistakes that help us learn so we can make different and better "good mistakes" next time.)

Each of the 45 chapters includes 30 or more questions, 10 or more targeted vocabulary words, a few proverbs, and 10 or more quotations. Although designed for advanced students, intermediate ESL students will find plenty of material to use and can benefit from exposure to the new words, phrases, and questions.

Each chapter focuses on a promising conversation topic. The questions allow the reader to practice exchanging experiences and ideas in a natural style. You can add questions, skip questions, and move on to related topics. Each chapter begins with easier questions and moves on to questions that are more abstract. Both native and non-native speakers will find the questions allow one to share experiences, exchange insights, and reflect on life.

A NOTE ON TERMS

ESL, short for English as a Second Language, remains the most common term in the United States—especially in public education.

TESOL, the largest professional organization, stands for Teachers of English to Speakers of Other Languages. Many scholars prefer to break down the field into sub-categories such as:

EFL: English as a Foreign Language

ESP: English for Special Purposes

ELT: English Language Teaching, and

ELL: English Language Learners.

We use ESL for both simplicity and convenience since we live in the United States.

The questions are conversation starters, and not scripts to follow. The goal remains to create a real dialogue, increase your understanding of your classmates, and gently push you toward using a richer vocabulary in your English conversations.

Many of these conversation worksheets were originally developed for an Advanced Conversation class that met four hours a week, 15 weeks a semester. The original college course textbook offered little more than vocabulary lists, cost too much, and avoided any topic that might cause any controversy. Several lessons talked about the weather, colors, etc. So I dropped the book, and created conversation worksheets with 30 related questions on practical topics for adult students. I didn't come in with a set point of view; I wanted to find out what people had experienced and their reflections on their lives, current events, and the bigger questions about our changing world. Why should we just talk about the weather and become bored when we could explore our lives, times, passions, and challenges?

Many students would contribute proverbs during our discussions since proverbs, sayings, and idioms can be useful in daily life. Often similar ideas, like "the sky is always blue somewhere", can be found across cultures. Proverbs can point out some universal aspects of the human experience— in 21st century America, 19th century England, 17th century Paris, 4th century China, or 1st century Rome. Proverbs may often contradict each other, yet the trick is to use the right proverb at the right time in the right situation. Sometimes it's good to know, and even hold, two opposite ideas. "Where you stand, depends on where you sit." Therefore, each chapter includes a proverb section.

This collection of proverbs and quotations also includes many insights from religious leaders and philosophers that go back even more than 2,000 years such as Buddha, Confucius, Aristotle, and the Biblical prophets. These quotations remind us that some conversations have spanned centuries and cultures. The selected quotations present a wide range of ideas, beliefs, and perspectives. Some quotations might make you laugh, some might make you sigh, and a few might even annoy you. Share your genuine feelings and reasons. Join the conversation. Free speech remains a rare and precious right.

Including classic quotations also helps preserve the insights and comments of well-known and significant cultural figures. This habit helps us escape the too-common delusion that the world began when we were born and provides a larger perspective. Sometimes knowing the speaker and historical era invites another way of looking at our modern lives.

Your English may not be perfect yet, but daily practice does lead to significant progress. Compelling Conversations gives you the tools and phrases to talk more and listen better to friends and strangers in English.

Finally, I hope you enjoy creating many compelling conversations!

Eric H. Roth
eric@compellingconversations.com

A few more tips for satisfying conversations with your partners:

• Be active

• Be curious

• Be encouraging

• Be kind

• Be open

• Be tolerant

• Make good mistakes

• Be yourself

Contents

"In America, nobody says you have to keep circumstances somebody else gives you."

AMY TAN
(1952–), Chinese-American novelist

your Life

1

GETTING STARTED

Proverbs and quotations appear frequently throughout this text. Reading the ideas of other people and other cultures helps you look at many ways of thinking and introduces you to some famous people.

Also, throughout these lessons, you will be asked to work with others. You will be asking questions about their experiences, and you will be answering questions which they ask you. In this way, you will be practicing English, learning about other cultures, and practicing ways to make conversation pleasant and interesting. Our goal is to create compelling conversations.

ACTIVITY ONE

Divide into groups of four. In conversation, it is often helpful to show other people that we understand what they are trying to communicate. A smile, a nod of the head, and eye contact are encouraging to others and invite them to continue. Frowning, shaking one's head no, or looking away while others are speaking will discourage others from trying.

In this class, we want to encourage others. In your groups, practice smiling at others and encouraging them. Take turns telling why you want to learn more English. Where do you speak English now? Where would you like to speak English more? Why?

ACTIVITY TWO

Words can also show that we want others to feel comfortable speaking. In your group, take turns saying each of the following statements. Give eye contact to others as you speak. This practice will make it easier to use these encouraging statements in your conversations with others.

- That is interesting.
- You are right!
- I enjoy listening to what you have to say.
- I like that!

- What happened next?
- Can you explain more?
- Please continue.
- Cool

NOTES & QUESTIONS

....

....

....

....

....

....

....

ACTIVITY THREE

In your group, read aloud each of the following quotations. Decide among yourselves what you think the quotation means. Then, talk about how the meaning of the quotation will help you work well with the other students in this class. Remember to practice using encouraging gestures and words with each other.

1. "Courtesy costs nothing."
   —Ralph Waldo Emerson (1803–1882), American writer, philosopher

2. "Pleasant words are as a honeycomb, sweet to the soul and health to the bones."
   —Bible

3. "You catch more flies with honey than with vinegar."
   —Proverb

4. "I hear and I forget. I see and I remember. I do and I understand."
   —Chinese proverb

5. "We learn by doing."
   —English proverb

6. "The secret of education is respecting the pupil."
   —Ralph Waldo Emerson (1803–1882), American poet, philosopher

7. "It is not best that we should all think alike; it is a difference of opinion which makes horse races."
   —Mark Twain (1835–1910), American writer, humorist

8. "I am tomorrow, or some future day, what I establish today. I am today what I established yesterday or some previous day."
   —James Joyce (1882–1941) Irish novelist

VOCABULARY

Please circle the words that you know. Ask your partner or teacher for the meanings of the other words.

quotation...

proverb ....

conversation ....

pleasant ....

gesture ....

nod ....

communicate ....

courage ....

discourage ....

encourage ....

argue ....

disagree ....

ACTIVITY FOUR

With the other members in your group, make a list of five or more important rules to follow which will help you have pleasant conversations in this class.

1. ....
2. ....
3. ....
4. ....
5. ....

THE CONVERSATION CONTINUES

Take turns reading the following quotations out loud. Pick a favorite.

1. "Conversation means being able to disagree and still continue the conversation."
   —Dwight MacDonald (1906–1982), American editor

2. "Speech is civilization itself...It is silence which isolates."
   —Thomas Mann (1875–1955), German writer

3. "If it is language that makes us human, one half of language is to listen."
   —Jacob Trapp (1899–1992) American religious leader

4. "Argument is the worst form of conversation."
   —Jonathon Swift (1667–1745), English writer, satirist

5. "People have one thing in common: they are all different."
   —Robert Zend (1929–1985), American writer

6. "Do what you can, with what you have, where you are."
   —Theodore Roosevelt (1858–1919), 26th U.S. President

7. "Talk low, talk slow, and don't say too much."
   —John Wayne (1907–1979), American actor

8. "Keep it light, bright and polite."
   —English proverb

9. "Man's main task in life is to give birth to himself."
   —Erich Fromm (1900–1980), psychologist

10. "There is only one beautiful child in the world, and each mother has that one."
    —Latin American proverb

11. "Life shrinks or expands in proportion to one's courage."
    —Anaïs Nin (1903–1977), French-American author

12. "Man does not speak because he thinks; he thinks because he speaks. Or rather, speaking is no different than thinking: to speak is to think."
    —Octavio Paz, (1914–1998), Mexican writer, Nobel Prize winner

ON YOUR OWN

People communicate with words 24 hours a day, seven days a week. During the next 24 hours, please carefully observe people talking to each other .

Note their communication style, gestures, and word choices. You can watch people in stores, on buses, at school and even on TV. Go head, be a spy!

Prepare to share three observations with the class.

1. ....

....

2. ....

....

3. ....

....

2
GOING BEYOND HELLO

TELLING YOUR STORY

Please interview the person sitting next to you. Feel free to add or skip any questions that you want. Take turns talking, jot down some notes, and prepare to introduce your partner to our class. Let's begin!

1. What's your full name? How do you spell that?

2. Who chose your name? Why?

3. Where were you born? Were you the first child? Second? Fifth?

4. Do you have any older brothers? Sisters? Younger siblings?

5. Where did you grow up? Is that a city, village, or suburb?

6. How would you describe yourself as a child? Why?

7. When did you decide to move to the U.S.? Why?

8. How long have you been in the United States?

9. Did you move here by yourself? How was the trip?

10. What possessions did you bring with you?
    Why did you choose these objects?

11. Can you share some of your first impressions of U.S.?

12. Do you have a favorite color? Number? Season? Why?

13. What kind of music do you listen to?
    Do you have a favorite singer? Group?

14. What's your favorite radio station or television channel? Why?

15. Can you recommend any movies to rent or see?
    Why do you like those films?

VOCABULARY

Please circle the words that you know. Ask your partner or teacher for the meanings of the other words.

interview ....

sibling...

suburb ....

possession...

impression ....

hobby ....

smile ....

frown ....

enthusiasm ....

goals ....

PROVERBS

Read the proverbs below. Can you add another saying?

Strangers are just friends you haven't met yet.—American

Beauty is a good letter of recommendation.—German

You never get a second chance to make a first impression.—American

You're never too old to learn.—Latin

A single conversation across the table with a
wise person is worth a month's study of books.—Chinese

THE CONVERSATION CONTINUES...

1. What do you like to do outside? Why?

2. Where do you walk, hike, jog, or bike on the weekends?

3. What's your favorite sport? Why?

4. How do you like to spend your free time? What interests you?

5. Do you have a hobby? How long have you enjoyed it?

6. How long have you studied English? Where?

7. Where do you usually speak English? Who do you usually talk with?

8. What's your best language? Where do you usually speak it? Why?

9. What makes you smile? Where do you feel most comfortable?

10. What are some things that might cause you to frown?

11. How do you express enthusiasm in a word or sound in your native language?

12. Do you have a favorite English word or expression? Why?

13. What are your goals for this year? Why? What's your plan?

14. How would your friends describe you? What would you add?

15. What are three things that you appreciate about living in the United States?

REMEMBER...
Be encouraging
Be kind
Be open

Which quotation is your favorite? Why?

1. "I never met a man I didn't like."
   —Will Rogers (1879–1935), American humorist

2. "I am free of all prejudices. I hate every one equally."
   —W. C. Fields (1880–1946), comedian

3. "There is no such thing as a worthless conversation, provided you know what to listen for. And questions are the breath of life for a conversation."
   —James Nathan Miller, contemporary journalist

4. "He's the sort of guy if you say, 'Hi ya, Clark, how are you?' he's stuck for an answer."
   —Ava Gardner, film star, describing her ex-lover, the film star Clark Gable.

5. "Conversation is an art in which a man has all mankind for his competitors, for it is that which all are practicing every day while they live."
   —Ralph Waldo Emerson (1803–1882), American essayist/philosopher

6. "Don't tell your friends about your indigestion. 'How are you' is a greeting, not a question."
   —Arthur Guiterman (1871–1943), American poet

7. "The true spirit of conversation consists in building on another man's observation, not overturning it."
   —Edward G. Bulwer-Lytton (1803–1873), British novelist/politician

8. "Confidence contributes more to conversation than wit."
   —Francois de La Rochefoucauld (1613–1680), French writer

9. "It takes two to speak truth—one to speak and another to hear."
   —Henry David Thoreau (1817–1862), American philosopher

10. "There is no such thing as conversation. It is an illusion. There are interesting monologues, that's all."
    —Rebecca West (1892–1983), English writer

11. "I am simple, complex, generous, selfish, unattractive, beautiful, lazy and driven."
    —Barbara Streisand (1942–), American singer, actress, director, producer

12. "Everything becomes a little different as soon as it is spoken out loud."
    —Hermann Hesse (1877–1962), novelist

13. "Never let your fear of striking out get in your way."
    —Babe Ruth (1895–1948), American baseball legend

14. "It was impossible to get a conversation going; everybody was talking too much."
    —Yogi Berra (1925–) legendary baseball manager/catcher

ON YOUR OWN

Before next class, compliment three people. Tell your class partner what happened.

3

BEING HOME

SHARING EXPERIENCES

Everybody lives somewhere. Share the story of your home with a conversation partner by responding to these questions. Feel free to add other questions.

1. Do you live in a house or an apartment?

2. How long have you lived there?

3. Why did you choose your current home?
   What attracted you?

4. Did you have a checklist when looking for a home?
   What was on it?

5. What legal documents did you have to sign before moving in?
   Lease? Mortgage? Other? Did you have to pay any fees?

6. What do you like about it?
   How long did it take you make a decision?

7. What do you dislike about it?
   What, if anything, annoys you?

8. Which is your favorite room? Why?
   What does it look like?

9. Which room is the heart of your current home?
   Kitchen? TV room?

10. What changes have you made to this residence? Paint? Repairs?

11. What further changes would you like to make?

12. What paintings, posters, or other artwork do you have?

13. Do you have any pets? What's their favorite spot?

14. What, if any plants or flowers, do you have? Where are they?

15. By the way, how did you find your current home?
    Word of mouth? Ad?

VOCABULARY

Which words do you already know? Working with your partner, use each of the vocabulary words in a sentence.

checklist...

lease...

mortgage..

fees...

repairs..

hardware..

artwork...

neighborhood..

neighbors...

prefer...

residence..

current...

interior...

homesick..

suburb..

appliances..

SAYINGS

What do these proverbs and sayings mean? Discuss them with your partner. Circle your favorite.

Home is where the heart is.

You can't go home again.

Home is where we grumble the most and are treated the best.

Birds return to old nests.—Japanese

A house is not a home.

Mi casa es su casa.—Spanish

THE CONVERSATION CONTINUES...

1. When you were a child, did you live in a house or an apartment?

2. How long did you live in one residence?

3. What did you like about it? What did you dislike?

4. With whom did you live as a child?

5. Which was your favorite room? Why?

6. Which room was the heart of your childhood home?

7. Have you ever felt homesick? What did you miss the most?

8. What is your favorite childhood memory at home?

9. Is your old neighborhood the same today as it was when you were a child?

10. Would you like to live there now? Why or why not?

11. Would you rather live in an apartment or a house? Why?

12. Would you rather live in a city, a suburb, a small town, or the country? Why?

13. Can you suggest some places to find interior design ideas?

14. What would your dream residence be like? Can you describe it in detail?

15. What modern appliances would your dream house have?

16. What makes a house or an apartment a home?

QUOTATIONS

Please read and review these quotations in a small group. Discuss what each one means. Then label a quote you like and one you dislike.

1. "He is happiest, be he king or peasant, who finds peace in his home."—Johann Wolfgang von Goethe (1749–1832), German playwright

2. "Anger in a home is like rottenness in a fruit."—Talmud

3. "A man's house is his castle." —Sir Edward Coke (1552–1634), English lord

4. Home: "The place where when you have to go there, they have to take you in."—Robert Frost (1875–1963), American poet

5. "Be it ever so humble, there's no place like home." —John Howard Payne (1791–1852), American lyricist

6. "A man builds a fine house; and now he has a master, and a task for life: he is to furnish, watch, show it, and keep it in repair, the rest of his days."—Ralph Waldo Emerson (1803–1882), American writer

7. "A man travels the world over in search of what he needs, and returns home to find it." —George Moore (1852–1933), Irish playwright

8. "No matter under what circumstances you leave it, home does not cease to be home. No matter how you lived there—well or poorly." —Joseph Brodsky (1940–1996), Russian-American Nobel winner

9. "Home is the girl's prison and the woman's workhouse."—George Bernard Shaw (1856–1950), Irish playwright and Nobel winner

10. "A woman should be home with the children, building that home and making sure there's a secure family atmosphere." —Mel Gibson (1956–), film director, actor

11. "The best way to keep children at home is make the home atmosphere pleasant, and let the air out of the tires." —Dorothy Parker (1893–1967), American writer

12. "Modern apartments are built on the principle that half as much room should cost twice as much money." —Evan Esar (1899–1995), American humorist

13. "Peace and rest at length have come, All the day's long toil is past, And each heart is whispering, Home, Home at last!" —Thomas Hood (1798–1845), English poet

ON YOUR OWN

Select five adjectives (spacious, cozy) for your dream home:

1. ....

2. ....

3. ....

4. ....

5. ....

Before the next class, find a home or apartment building that you would like to live in.

Bring a specific address to class. Describe the building to your group.

4
DESCRIBING FAMILY TIES

SHARING EXPERIENCES

Family remains the center of society. Share your experiences and discover your partner's diverse experiences as a family member.

1. Do you have a large, medium, or small family? How many people are in your family?

2. What are your parents' names? How do you spell their names?

3. Where were your parents born? Were they born in a hospital? Elsewhere?

4. How did your parents meet? What attracted them to each other?

5. How long did they know each other before they got married?

6. Do you know how old your parents were when they got married?

7. How many siblings do you have? Are you the oldest? Youngest?

8. What do you enjoy doing with your siblings?

9. While living in your homeland, did you live with your nuclear family or your extended family? With whom do you live now?

10. Does your extended family have a leader or dominant figure? Is there a patriarch or a matriarch?

11. How many aunts and uncles do you have?

12. Which aunt or uncle is your favorite? Why?

13. What language or languages did you hear in your childhood home? Which languages are spoken now?

14. Do you exchange gifts on holidays? Which holidays?

15. Who gives the best gifts in your family? Why?

16. What do you appreciate about your family?

17. How can families provide comfort?

Please circle the words that you know. Ask your partner or teacher for the meanings of the other words.

sibling...

spouse..

nuclear family ....

blended family ....

extended family ....

reunion..

matriarch ....

patriarch...

stepsister..

ancestor..

half-brother ....

in-laws..

PROVERBS

Read the common sayings and proverbs below. Can you add one more?

Half of your fortune lies in your family line.—Korean

Of all the virtues, family duty is the first.—Chinese

A brother helped by a brother is like a fortified city.—Book of Proverbs

Like father, like son.—Latin

Like mother, like daughter.—Persian

Whoever marries for money will have unworthy children.—Talmud

THE CONVERSATION CONTINUES...

1. What days were special for your family when you were a child?

2. Which relative do you feel closest to?

3. What makes that relationship special?

4. Whom do you respect the most in your family? Why?

5. Does your family hold reunions? Can you describe a recent one?

6. How do you keep in touch with distant relatives? Do you use email?

7. How many times has your family moved? Why?

8. Could you describe some of your favorite family photographs?

9. Is divorce legal in your homeland? Are there particular conditions required for divorce? What are they? Any other restrictions?

10. Why are "blended families" more common today?

11. What might cause someone to become a "black sheep" in a family?

12. What things might parents keep secret from their children?

13. What things might children keep secret from their parents?

REMEMBER...

Be yourself

Skip awkward questions

Add natural questions

14. Do you have any step or half brothers or sisters? Do you think these relationships are harder? Why?

15. What rivalries has your family had? Have you felt any rivalry with relatives?

16. How can families create stress?

17. What were some important events in your family history?

18. Which ancestor would you most like to meet? Why?

19. How are family habits and traditions different in the United States than in your native land?

20. What are your suggestions for stronger and healthier relationships?

QUOTATIONS

Which quotation is your favorite? Why?

1. "All happy families resemble one another; every unhappy family is unhappy in its own fashion."
   —Leo Tolstoy in *Anna Karenina* (1828–1910), Russian novelist

2. "All that I am or hope to be, I owe to my angel mother."
   —Abraham Lincoln (1809–1865), 16th U.S. President

3. "We never know the love of a parent until we become parents ourselves."
   —Henry Ward Beecher (1813–1887), clergyman/abolitionist

4. "Rearing a family is probably the most difficult job in the world."
   —Virginia Satir (1916–1988), family therapist

5. "Heredity is what sets the parents of a teenager wondering about each other."—Laurence J. Peter (1919–1990) educator and author

6. "Nobody can do for little children what grandparents do. Grandparents sort of sprinkle stardust over the lives of little children."
   —Alex Haley (1921–1992), American novelist and biographer

7. "The greatest thing in family life is to take a hint when a hint is intended—and not to take a hint when a hint isn't intended."
   —Robert Frost (1874–1963), American poet

8. "We must learn to live together as brothers or perish as fools."
   —Dr. Martin Luther King (1929–1968), Nobel Peace Prize recipient

9. "The family that prays together stays together."
   —Slogan of Father Patrick Peyton's Family Rosary Radio Crusade

10. "When you are a mother, you are never really alone in your thoughts. A mother always has to think twice, once for herself and once for her child."
    —Sophia Loren (1934–), Italian actress

11. "Is solace anywhere more comforting than that in the arms of a sister?"—Alice Walker (1944–), American novelist and poet

12. "The first duty of love is to listen."
    —Paul Tillich (1886–1965), theologian

ON YOUR OWN

Make a Family Tree back to your grandparents and, if you have children, including your children.

Give birth dates if they are known and death dates if a person has deceased.

Prepare to share with your class partner.

5
EATING AND DRINKING

SHARING TASTES

Everybody eats. Food is both a necessity and a pleasure, and remains a safe and interesting way to learn more about people. Interview your partner and share your eating and drinking experiences.

1. Do you consider eating a chore, a duty, or a pleasure? Why?

2. What did you eat yesterday? Was it a typical day?

3. Do you drink juice/tea/coffee in the morning?
   Regular or decaffeinated?

4. Do you eat at the same time each day?
   Or do you eat when you have time?

5. Do you prefer salty snacks or sweet snacks?
   How often do you have snacks?

6. Where do you usually shop for food?
   What shopping tips can you share?

7. What drinks do you often have with your evening meal?

8. What kind of meat do you enjoy eating? Beef? Pork? Poultry? Fish?

9. What is your favorite vegetable? Are you a vegetarian?

10. What is your favorite fruit? Which fruits do you find delicious?

11. Can you name three American dishes that you really enjoy or savor?

12. Has your diet changed since moving to the United States? How?

13. Which dishes from your country would you recommend to a tourist?

14. Is there any food you enjoyed in your homeland that you haven't found here?

15. Are you a chef?

16. What's your favorite recipe? Where did you get it?
    What dishes do you cook?

VOCABULARY

Please circle the words that you know. Write three questions using them.

decaffeinated...

chef ....

fast..

famished...

feast ....

gluttony ....

famine ....

vegetarian ....

culinary ....

savor ....

edible ....

NOTES & QUESTIONS

....

....

....

....

....

....

....

IDIOMS, PUNS, AND EXPRESSIONS

Which is your favorite?

I'm on a seafood diet. I see food and I eat it.

She loves candy, ice cream, and cookies. She has a sweet tooth.

A boiled egg in the morning is hard to beat.

Eat, drink, and be merry.

The most sincere love is the love of food.

THE CONVERSATION CONTINUES...

1. What is your favorite restaurant? In what language do you order?

2. How often do you eat at a fast food restaurant? Why?

3. Are American fast food chains popular in your homeland? Why?

4. In your native land, did all members of your family eat the evening meal together? Who cooked the food? Who served the food?

5. In your native country, what foods or drinks are associated with weddings? Birthdays? Funerals?

6. What foods or drinks are associated with holy days or national holidays?

7. Have you ever eaten at a feast? When? What meals remind you of happy times?

8. Have you ever fasted? Why? Were you famished after skipping two meals?

9. Does your religion have dietary rules or restrictions? What are they?

10. Has there ever been a famine in your native country? What caused it?

11. Have you ever tried to diet to lose weight? What did you do?

12. Can you name several types of diets?

13. Is your diet restricted in any way by health considerations? How?

14. Do you ever read food labels? Do you have any food allergies?

15. What meals does your family share? Who cooks? Who serves?

16. Does your family share recipes? Which recipe would you like?

17. Would you like to share a favorite recipe?

18. Are you adventurous in seeking out new culinary delights?

19. What is your ideal dinner? Please describe the dishes, the guests, and the location.

QUOTATIONS

Circle the quotations that you like.

1. "Better beans and bacon in peace than cakes and ale in fear."
   —Aesop (ca. 550 B.C.)

2. "The proof of the pudding is in the eating. By a small sample, we may judge the whole of a piece"
   —Miguel De Cervantes (1547–1616), Spanish writer

3. "The satiated man and the hungry one do not see the same thing when they look upon a loaf of bread."
   —Rumi (1207–1273), Persian poet and mystic

4. "More die in the United States of too much food than of too little."—John Kenneth Galbraith (1908–) ambassador, economist

5. "Live. Love. Eat."—Wolfgang Puck (1949–), chef

6. "When I drink, I think; and when I think, I drink."
   —Francois Rabelais (1495–1553), satirist

7. "Edible (adj). Good to eat and wholesome to digest, as a worm to a toad, a toad to a snake, a snake to a pig, a pig to a man, and a man to a worm."—Ambrose Bierce (1842–1916), American writer

8. "I have taken more out of alcohol than alcohol has taken out of me."—Winston Churchill (1874–1965), British Prime Minister, Nobel Prize winner

9. "The secret of staying young is to live honestly, eat slowly, and lie about your age."
   —Lucille Desiree Ball (1911–1984), American TV star and actress

10. "People who drink to drown their sorrow should be told that sorrow knows how to swim."
    —Ann Landers (1918–2002), American advice columnist

11. "I went on a diet, swore off drinking and heavy eating, and in fourteen days I lost two weeks."
    —Joe E. Louis (1914–1981), world boxing champion

12. "I thought, I called, I planned, I shopped, I schlepped, I cleaned, I chopped, I soaked, I peeled, I rinsed, I grated, I minced, I simmered, I larded, I mixed, I fried, I boiled, I baked, I sauted, I souffleed, I flame boiled, and I sweated. So, tell me it's great!"
    —Slogan on a novelty kitchen apron in the United States

13. "If it's beautifully arranged on the plate, you know someone's fingers have been all over it."—Julia Child (1912–2004), American chef/author

ON YOUR OWN

Write menu descriptions for your perfect meal. Include the major ingredients of dishes as one finds on a menu.

Be sure to include appetizers, beverages and desserts. Indulge yourself.

Now describe your delicious choices to your group.

....

....

....

....

....

....

....

....

6

EXPLORING DAILY HABITS

SHARING STORIES

Do you know your own habits? Share stories about your habits and find out more about your partner's habits in a friendly exchange.

1. How many hours of sleep do you usually get?
   Is that enough sleep for you?

2. Do you usually use an alarm clock to wake up?
   How often do you oversleep?

3. What time do you usually get up in the morning?
   Do you get up with the sun?

4. Do you jump out of bed? Are you a morning monster?

5. Can you describe your morning habits? Are you in a hurry?

6. What do you eat for breakfast? What do you prefer to drink in the morning?

7. Can you describe a typical summer afternoon for you?
   A winter afternoon?

8. How did you come to school today?
   Did you arrive by foot, by bus, or by car?

9. How long is your daily commute to work or school?

10. What's your daily schedule like? Busy? Slow? Loose? Full?

11. What was your daily schedule like five years ago?
    How is different now?

12. Do you do many things at the last minute? Why?

13. In your daily life, what modern appliances or machines do you use?

14. What task or chore have you put off or postponed?

15. In what kind of stores do you prefer to shop for clothes? Thrift? Upscale? Modern? Department? Mall? Mom and Pop? Why?

16. Where do you like buying your groceries? Why?
    What do you usually buy?

VOCABULARY

Please circle the words that you know. Use them to write four sentences.

curious..

habits..

oversleep ....

routine..

schedule ....

tend to ....

disciplined ....

addict ....

lifestyle ....

impulsive ....

consumer ....

PROVERBS

Read the common sayings and proverbs below. Can you add two more?

The more you chew your meat, the better it tastes;
The more you speak, the lighter your heart becomes.—Korean

An old cat will never learn to dance.—Moroccan

Habits are first cobwebs, then cables.—Spanish

Love makes marriage possible,
and habit makes it endurable.—American

The fool in a hurry drinks his tea with chopsticks.—Chinese

(Add yours) ....

(Add yours) ....

REMEMBER...
Be curious

Be open

Be tolerant

THE CONVERSATION CONTINUES...

1. What kind of consumer are you? A bargain hunter? Impulsive buyer?

2. What are your TV viewing habits? Do you always watch certain shows? Which ones?

3. How often do you use a computer? When do you send email?

4. Do you find the daily lifestyle in the United States hectic? Can you give some examples?

5. What are some dangerous or unhealthy addictions?

6. Why do you think so many people are addicted to alcohol and illegal drugs?

7. Do you consider smoking a bad habit? Why?

8. In what ways are you self-disciplined?

9. Are you lazy in any ways? How?

10. Do you tend to see the glass as half-full or half-empty? Are you more of an optimist or a pessimist? Why?

11. What is your favorite time of day? Why?

12. How do your weekends differ from your Monday-Friday routine?

13. What are some of your healthier habits?

14. What are some of your less healthy habits?

15. How do your habits compare to your parents' habits at your age?

16. Have your daily habits changed since moving to the United States?

17. Given a choice, would you prefer to live now or 100 years ago? Why?

QUOTATIONS

Which quotation is your favorite? Why?

1. "Nothing is in reality either pleasant or unpleasant by nature; but all things become so through habit."
—Epictetus (55–135), Greek stoic philosopher

2. "Men's natures are alike; it is their habits that separate them."
—Confucius (551–479 B.C.E.) great Chinese philosopher

3. "We are what we repeatedly do. Excellence, then, is not an act, but a habit."—Aristotle (384–322 B.C.E.), Ancient Greek philosopher

4. "Habit and character are closely interwoven, habit becoming like a second nature."
—Moses Maimonides (1135–1204), Jewish philosopher

5. "Don't let your sins turn into bad habits."
—Saint Theresa (1873–1897), French nun and author

6. "Nothing so needs reforming as other people's habits."
—Mark Twain (1835–1910), American humorist and novelist

7. "Habit for him was all the test of truth; 'It must be right: I've done it from my youth."—George Crabbe (1754–1832), English poet

8. "The perpetual obstacle to human advancement is custom."
—John Stuart Mill (1806–1873), English political philosopher

9. "The chains of habit are too weak to be felt until they are too strong to be broken."
—Dr. Samuel Johnson (1709–1784), English author

10. "Habit is habit, and not to be flung out of the window by any man, but coaxed downstairs a step at a time."
—Mark Twain (1835–1910), American humorist

11. "Habit will reconcile us to everything but change."
—Charles Caleb Colton (1780–1832), English writer and collector

12. "Any man who reads too much and uses his own brain too little falls into lazy habits of thinking."
—Albert Einstein (1879–1955), scientist and *Time* magazine's Man of the 20th Century

13. "For many, negative thinking is a habit, which over time, becomes an addiction."
—Peter McWilliams (1949–2000) American self-help author

14. "The unfortunate thing about this world is that good habits are so much easier to give up than bad ones."
—Somerset Maugham (1874–1965), English novelist

ON YOUR OWN

Keep an activity log for a day. Share it with your conversation partner.

7

BEING YOURSELF

SHARING PERSPECTIVES

From consulting charts and reading palms to taking personality tests and reading self-help books, people love to describe themselves.

1. Which three adjectives would you use to describe your personality?

2. Are you shy or outgoing? When are you most outgoing?

3. Are you daring or cautious? In what ways?

4. Are you usually patient or impatient? Can you give an example?

5. Are you quiet or talkative? When are you most talkative? Least?

6. Would you call yourself a leader or a follower? Why?

7. Are you generous or selfish? Are you too selfish or over generous?

8. In what ways are you rigid? In what ways are you flexible?

9. In what ways are you traditional? In what ways are you modern?

10. If pessimistic is 1 and optimistic is 10, what would your number be on the scale? Why did you decide on that number?

11. On a scale of 1-10, how assertive are you?

12. Is your personality more like your mother or your father? In what ways?

13. Which color would you use to describe your personality?

14. Which animal would you use to describe yourself? Tiger? Mouse? Why?

15. Do you believe in astrology? Which sign are you in the zodiac? Does the pattern of this sign match your personality?

16. Which animal year are you according to Chinese astrology? Does this fit?

17. Have you ever taken a personality test from a magazine or online? Was it helpful? Was it fun? Was it accurate?

18. Which season of the year best describes your personality? In what ways?

Please circle the words that you know. Ask your partner or teacher for the meanings of the other words.

character ....

patient ....

talkative ....

generous ....

rigid ....

flexible ....

autumn ....

zodiac ....

accurate ....

optimist ....

pessimist ....

nurture ....

THE CONVERSATION CONTINUES...

1. Do you think our personalities are set when we are born?

2. Can we change our personalities? How?

3. How has your personality changed in the last ten years?

4. Which three words would you use to describe the personality of your best friend?

5. How are your personalities similar?
   How are your personalities different?

6. Why do you think opposites are sometimes attracted to each other?

7. Some cultures define personality in terms of the elements: Would you say you are primarily air, water, fire, or earth? Why did you choose that element?

8. Which three qualities do you think of as yin (feminine)?

9. Which three qualities do you think of as yang (masculine)?

10. Can you name one yin quality and one yang quality which describe you?

11. How might being raised in poverty influence someone's personality?

12. Do you think being born in extreme wealth would change your personality? How?

13. If you had been born in another country, do you think your personality would be different? How?

14. Can you think of somebody with a good personality and bad character?

15. What is the difference between one's personality and one's character?

REMEMBER...

Be encouraging

Make good mistakes

Be yourself

16. Are you primarily an extrovert or an introvert? Why do you say that?

17. Do you think nature (biology) or nurture (our circumstances) are more important in shaping our personalities? Why do you say that?

18. What are your best qualities?

QUOTATIONS

Circle the quotations you like.

1. "Know thyself."
   —Socrates, Greek philosopher (470–399 B.C. E.)

2. "The man of character bears the accidents of life with dignity and grace, making the best of circumstances."
   —Aristotle (384–322 B.C.E.), Greek philosopher and scientist

3. "This above all: To thine own self be true, And it must follow, as the night the day, Thou canst not then be false to any man."
   —William Shakespeare, playwright (1564–1616)

4. "Character is much easier kept than recovered."
   —Thomas Paine (1737–1809), writer and revolutionary

5. "It is absurd to divide people into good and bad. People are either charming or tedious."
   —Oscar Wilde (1856–1900), English playwright

6. "Some people with great virtues are disagreeable, while others with great vice are delightful."
   —Duc de la Rochefoucauld (1613—1680), French philosopher

7. "The meeting of two personalities is like the contact of two chemical substances; if there is any reaction, both are transformed."
   —Carl Jung (1875–1961), Swiss psychiatrist

8. "The Doc told me that I had a dual personality. Then he lays an $82 bill on me, so I give him 41 bucks and say, 'Get the other 41 bucks from the other guy.' "
   —Jerry Lewis (1926–), American comedian

9. "I am what is mine. Personality is the original personal property.
   —Norman O. Brown (1913–2002), American scholar

10. "Man's main task in life is to give birth to himself, to become what he potentially is. The most important product of his effort is his own personality."
    —Erich Fromm (1900–1980), American psychologist

11. "I am absolutely convinced that no wealth in the world can help humanity forward. The example of great and fine personalities is the only thing that can lead us to fine ideas and noble deeds. Can anyone imagine Moses, Jesus, or Gandhi with the money bags of Carnegie?"
    —Albert Einstein (1879–1955), Nobel Prize winner in Physics

12. "Generous people are rarely mentally ill people."
    —Karl Menninger (1893–1990) American psychiatrist

ON YOUR OWN

What do you like about yourself?

Write a postcard to a stranger which celebrates yourself and your strongest traits.

8

STAYING HEALTHY

WALKING THE WALK

Sometimes it is easier to talk the talk about staying healthy than walking the walk to stay healthy. Interview your partner and exchange health tips.

1. What are some signs of being healthy?

2. What do your friends or relatives do to stay healthy?

3. What do you do to stay healthy?

4. Have your health habits changed in the last few years? How?

5. What is something that many people should do, but don't do to stay healthy?

6. Do you know any home remedies for common ailments?

7. How do you treat a sore throat? Minor cut? Headaches?

8. What are some causes of back pain?
   What are some possible remedies?

9. Do you take daily vitamins? Which ones? Why?

10. Do you regularly take over-the-counter drugs or prescription drugs? Why?

11. Is there a disease or condition which is common in your family? What steps have you taken to forestall or prevent this illness?

12. How often do you wash your hands? What other precautions do you take to prevent the spread of germs?

13. Do you eat healthy food? Do you have any unhealthy eating habits?

14. Do you enjoy smoking? What are some of the dangers of smoking?

15. How much sleep do you usually get?
    Is your sleep restful, or do you toss and turn?

16. How often do you feel tired or exhausted? What can you do to feel more energetic?

VOCABULARY

Circle the words that you already know. Look up the other words.

prevent ....

prevention ....

restrict ....

hygiene ....

germs ....

symptoms ....

operation ....

restriction ....

prescription ....

remedy ....

over-the-counter ....

exercise ....

meditation ....

medication ....

overcome ....

PROVERBS

What do these proverbs and sayings mean? Can you add another?

An apple a day keeps the doctor away.—English

Few desires, buoyant spirits; many cares, feeble health.—Chinese

A sick person is a prisoner.—Yemenite

He who has health has hope,
and he who has hope, has everything.—Arab

Nature, time, and patience are the three great physicians.—Irish

In the emergency room, we can ease their
pain, but we can not ease their lives.

Prevention beats medication.

Put a lid on what smells bad.—Japanese

Old age is a thousand headaches.—Persian

(Add yours) ....

1. Do you exercise regularly? What are your favorite exercises?

2. Do you take regular walks? Ride a bike? Go to the gym? Practice Tai Chi or yoga?

3. What can cause stomachaches? Do you eat quickly? Do you eat spicy foods?

4. Do you find yourself worrying a lot? Do you have ulcers?

5. Do you keep track of your blood pressure or cholesterol? How?

6. What are some warning signs for a heart attack? What do doctors recommend?

7. How is general health care easier in the United States than in your home country?

8. What inoculations or medical tests did you get before entering the United States?

9. Are there diseases that are common in your native country, but are rare in the United States? Which ones?

10. Are there common diseases in the U.S. which are rare in your homeland? Which ones?

11. Have you ever been to a hospital? Why? What made that visit memorable?

12. Are you at your ideal weight? Should you gain weight to attain your ideal? Should you lose weight to attain your ideal?

13. Do you restrict your diet for health reasons? How? Why?

14. Have you seen TV ads for prescription drugs? Do you trust the ads? Why or why not?

15. Do our emotions and thoughts affect our health? How?

16. Do you follow any regimen like meditation, yoga, or prayer to calm your mind and body?

17. What three things could you do to improve your general health?

NOTES & QUESTIONS

....

....

....

....

....

....

....

QUOTATIONS

Pick your favorite five quotations, and explain your choices.

1. "The secret of health for both mind and body is not to mourn for the past, not to worry about the future, not to anticipate troubles, but to live in the present moment wisely and earnestly."
   —Siddhartha Guatama (563–483 B.C.E.), philosopher

2. "The first duty of a physician is that he should do the sick no harm."
   —Hippocrates (460–380 B.C.E.), ancient Greek physician

3. "It is part of the cure to wish to be cured."
   —Seneca the Younger (4 B.C.E.–65 A.D.), Roman philosopher/statesmen

4. "Better use medicines at the outset than at the last moment."
   —Publilius Syrus (85–43 B.C.E.), Roman writer

5. "Body and spirit are twins: God only knows which is which."
   —Algernon Swinburne (1837–1909), English writer and critic

6. "A sound mind in a sound body is a short, but full description of a happy state in this world."
   —John Locke (1632–1704), English philosopher

7. "Early to bed and early to rise makes a man healthy, wealthy, and wise."
   —Benjamin Franklin (1706–1790), American icon

8. "Health is so necessary to all duties, as well as the pleasures of life, that the crime of squandering it is equal to folly."
   —Dr. Samuel Johnson (1709–1784), British writer

9. "You can't lose weight by talking about it. You have to keep your mouth shut."
   —The Old Farmer's Almanac

10. "You can't ignore the importance of a good digestion. The joy of life...depends on a sound stomach."
    —Joseph Conrad (1857–1924), English author

11. "There is no cure for birth or death save to enjoy the interval."
    —George Santayana (1863–1952), American philosopher

12. "The only way to keep your health is to eat what you don't want, drink what you don't like, and do what you'd rather not."
    —Mark Twain (1835–1910), American humorist

13. "Be careful about reading a health book. You may die of a misprint."
    —Mark Twain (1835–1910), American humorist

ON YOUR OWN

List your top five tips for staying healthy and happy. Prepare to share your advice with the class.

1. ....

2. ....

3. ....

4. ....

5. ....

9
PARENTING

SHARING EXPERIENCES

Everyone was once a child; most are or will become parents. Share your experiences and exchange ideas on parenting pleasures and challenges.

1. Where are you in your family's birth order?

2. How old were your parents when you were born?

3. Did your parents ever live with their parents?

4. When you were a baby, who was your primary caretaker?

5. What activities do you remember doing with your mother?

6. What activities do you remember doing with your father?

7. Do you remember playing with your parents? What did you play?

8. When you were a child, were you ever punished? How? Why?

9. Which of your parents was the main disciplinarian in your family?

10. Were the rules different for girls than for boys?
    What about family expectations for girls and boys?

11. Do you remember helping either of your parents with chores?
    Which ones?

12. Do you know any parents that hovered over their children like a helicopter? Why or why not?

13. What did your parents expect from you as a teenager?
    Did you rebel?

14. Which parenting duties do you think your parents did well?

15. What would you like to change about the way your parents treated you as a child? A teenager? Why?

16. Are you close with your father or mother now?
    What do you do together?

17. Do you resemble either of your parents? How?

18. What are you grateful to your parents for?

VOCABULARY

Circle the words that you know. Write three questions with them.

primary ....

duties..

caretaker ....

chores...

estranged...

protect ....

loyal..

sacrifice ....

spank...

qualities ....

resemble ....

ideal..

PROVERBS

Do you know these proverbs? What are some others about parenting?

Love your children with your heart,
but train them with your hands.—Ukrainian

Don't threaten a child; either punish him or forgive him.—Talmud

It's an ill bird that fouls its own nest.—Chinese

Emeralds and crystals glitter when lit.—Japanese

Spare the rod and spoil the child.—The Bible

THE CONVERSATION CONTINUES...

1. Are you especially close with any of your siblings?
   What do you do together?

2. Are you estranged from any of your siblings? Why?

3. Do you have children? What are their ages?

4. Can you briefly describe each of your children?
   What do they like to do?

5. Do you want children? How many?

6. In what ways do you hope to repeat the parenting skills of your
   father and mother? How would you describe their parenting style?

7. Are there also ways you hope to be a better parent than your
   parents? How?

8. When, if ever, do you discipline your children? What are some
   methods of discipline? Talking? Additional chores? Grounding?
   Spanking? What works best?

9. How do parents sacrifice for their children?
   Why isn't this always appreciated?

10. What do you think is the ideal age for parents to be? Why?

"When I was a boy of fourteen, my father was so ignorant I could hardly stand to have the old man around. But when I got to be twenty-one, I was astonished at how much he had learned in seven years."

Mark Twain (1835–1910) American humorist

REMEMBER...

Be kind

Be open

Be supportive

11. In what ways was it easier to be a parent 40 years ago? How was it more difficult?

12. What are some problems that parents face today?

13. What are some "good mistakes" that parents sometimes make?

14. What are some of the satisfactions of being a parent?

15. What movies have touched you by their depiction of parents and children?

16. How would you describe an ideal father? Ideal mother?

17. What five qualities would you like your children to have?

18. Can you share your top five tips for being a loving parent?

QUOTATIONS

Circle the quotations that you agree with.

1. "Children today are tyrants. They contradict their parents, gobble their food, and tyrannize their teachers."
   —Socrates (469–399 B.C.E.), Greek philosopher

2. "Obeying from love is better than obeying from fear."
   —Rashi (1040–1105), rabbi and scholar

3. "Give me the children until they are seven and anyone may have them afterwards."
   —Saint Francis Xavier (1506–1552), Catholic educator

4. "A child is not a vase to be filled, but a fire to be lit."
   —Rabelais (1494–1553) French essayist and humanist

5. "Before I got married, I had six theories about bringing up children. Now I have six children and no theories."
   —John Wilmot, Lord Rochester (1647–1680)

6. "The first half of our lives is ruined by our parents, and the second half by our children."
   —Clarence Darrow (1857–1938) American lawyer

7. "No two children are ever born into the same family."
   —Leo Rosten (1908–1997) American writer

8. "Insanity is hereditary; you can get it from your children."
   —Sam Levenson, (1911–1980) American humorist and journalist

9. "The children have been a wonderful gift to me, and I'm thankful to have once again seen the world through their eyes."
   —Jacqueline Kennedy Onassis (1929–1994) first lady

10. "No parent should ever have to choose between work and family; between earning a decent wage and caring for a child."
    —Bill Clinton (1946–) 42nd U.S. President

11. "In the final analysis, it is not what you do for your children, but what you have taught them to do for themselves that will make them successful human beings."
    —Ann Landers, (1918–2002) advice columnist

ON YOUR OWN

Interview a successful parent. What tips does that person offer?

OR

List five things you are grateful for.

1. ....

2. ....

3. ....

4. ....

5. ....

MAKING AND KEEPING FRIENDS

SHARING MEMORIES

We all want good friends. How does one make good friends? Share your ideas about friendship with your partner.

1. Did you have a best friend when you were an 8-year-old? Who?

2. What did you do together? Can you describe your best friend?

3. Who was your best friend when you were 14? What did you do?

4. Are you still friends, or pals, with the best friends of your youth?

5. Why do best friends sometimes drift apart?

6. What are some tips for keeping a friendship strong?

7. Who is your best friend now? How did you meet your best friend?

8. What activities do you do with your friend?
   What makes this friendship special?

9. What do you and your best friend have in common?

10. How are you and your best friend different?

11. Have you seen the TV show "Friends"? Do you like it? Who is your favorite character?

12. Can you think of a good movie about friendship?

13. In your opinion, are there rules for a friendship?

14. What are some things that a good friend should do?

15. Are there things that a good friend should not do? Like what?

16. Do you think you are a good friend to others? In what ways?

17. Do you think friends should loan each other money? Why or why not?

18. How do you deepen friendships? Can you share five tips for making and keeping friends?

19. Which of your friends would make good roommates? Why?

20. Do you have any friends that you would not want as roommates?

Use the words or phrases you know in sentences.

fast friends ....

pal ....

drift apart ....

crisis ....

opinion in common ....

circle of friends ....

betray ....

roommate ....

Googled ....

supportive ....

PROVERBS

Circle the proverbs with which you agree.

A friend in need is a friend indeed.—Latin

Never catch a falling knife or a falling friend.—Scottish

Do not protect yourself by a fence,
but rather by your friends.—Czech

Do not use a hatchet to remove a fly from your friend's face.—Chinese

Lend money to a good friend, and you will lose the
money as well as your friend.—Korean

Fate chooses your relatives; you choose your friends.—French

Your best friend is yourself.—American

Your best friend won't tell you.—Mouthwash ad

THE CONVERSATION CONTINUES...

1. Why do fast friends often form in crisis situations?

2. How do you meet new friends? Do you have any tips for making friends?

3. How do you keep in touch with friends?

4. Do you use instant messaging with friends?

5. Have you ever Googled a friend, coworker, or date?

6. Do you think that people of the opposite sex can be friends?

7. Have you ever had a good friend of the opposite sex?

8. Do you think one can truly be friends with former romantic partners?

9. Do you know a married couple who are best friends?

10. If so, why do you think that works?

11. Have you ever felt betrayed by a friend? How did you react?

12. Do you think it is fair to judge people by their friends? Why?

13. Do you have a close circle of friends? What unites you?

REMEMBER...

Be active

Be encouraging

Be curious

14. Can one be friends with one's parents? Why or why not?

15. Can one be friends with one's children? Why or why not?

16. Can you think of classic stories about true friendship?

QUOTATIONS

Read the quotations aloud. With your partner, decide what they mean. Then, circle the ones with which you agree.

1. "Without friends no one would choose to live, though he had all other goods."
   —Aristotle (384–322 B.C.E.), Greek philosopher

2. "Have no friends not equal to yourself."
   —Confucius (551–479 B.C.E.), Chinese philosopher

3. "A faithful friend is the medicine of life."
   —Ecclesiastes 6:16

4. "The shifts of Fortune test the reliability of friends."
   —Cicero (106–43 B.C.E.), Roman statesman

5. "It is more shameful to distrust our friends than to be deceived by them."
   —Duc de La Rochefoucauld (1613–1680)

6. "Don't walk behind me, I may not lead. Don't walk in front of me, I may not follow. Just walk beside me and be my friend."
   —Albert Camus (1913–1960), French novelist

7. "Each friend represents a world in us, a world possibly not born until they arrive, and it is only by this meeting that a new world is born."
   — Anaïs Nin (1903–1977) French-American author

8. "If a man does not make new acquaintances as he advances through life, he will soon find himself alone. A man should keep his friendships in constant repair. "
   —Samuel Johnson (1709–1784) English scholar

9. (A friend is) "Someone who will help you move; a good friend is someone who will help you move a body."
   —Alexei Sayle (1952–), British comedian and actor

10. "Animals are such agreeable friends; they ask no questions, they pass no criticisms."
    —George Eliot/Mary Ann Evans (1819–1880), English novel

11. "One's friends are that part of the human race with which one can be human."
    —George Santayana (1863–1952) philosopher

12. "It is easier to forgive an enemy than to forgive a friend."
    —William Blake (1757–1827), English poet

13. "Have friends. It's a second existence."
    —Baltasar Gracian, (1601–1658), Spanish philosopher

ON YOUR OWN

Write a letter, by hand or on a computer, to a friend that you have not communicated with recently. Feel free to include photos, etc.

Share it with your group.

11

LOVING DOGS AND OTHER PETS

SHARING MEMORIES

Please ask your partner about their dog or other pet. Take turns so the conversation flows. Encourage your partner.

1. Are you an animal lover or a pet person?
   Can I call you a "dog person"?

2. What is the name of your favorite pet? How did you choose it?

3. What does, or did, your favorite dog/pet look like?
   Can you describe your pet?

4. Can you tell me about your dog's personality?
   What makes this pet special for you?

5. How did your dog join your family?
   What were some factors in your decision?

6. What are your favorite photographs of your favorite dog?
   Are they displayed?

7. Did you train your dog? How? To do what? Why?

8. How do you take care of your dog? Give specific examples.

9. So, what makes a good pet owner or guardian?
   What are the tips and taboos?

10. How do you play with your dog (or other pet)?
    What do you enjoy doing together?

11. Does your dog like car trips? Beach walks? Hikes? Parks? Playing with Frisbees?

12. What else does your favorite pet like to do?

13. How did others in your family feel about your favorite dog/rabbit/fish/bird/other pet?

14. Why are dogs good pets? Do you agree that dogs are the ideal pet?

15. What are some challenges with having a dog?

16. What are some dog breeds that you think are beautiful? Strange?

VOCABULARY

Define the words you know.

personality ....

rescued ....

mutt ....

purebred ....

veterinarian ....

spayed ....

guardian ....

train ....

pamper ....

allergies ....

fashionable ....

dogma ....

IDIOMS

Do you know these common idioms? What do they mean?

His bark is worse than his bite.

It's raining cats and dogs.

She's sniffing the air before making a decision.

He's like a dog marking his territory.

PROVERBS

Can you think of another proverb about dogs?

Let sleeping dogs lie.—German

A dog is man's best friend.—English

Two dogs can kill a lion.—Jewish

(Add your own) ....

THE CONVERSATION CONTINUES...

1. What is a purebred? What's a mutt?

2. Have you ever owned a purebred dog? What kind?

3. Have you ever owned a mutt? What did your mutt look like?

4. When did you first get a dog? How old were you?

5. How do dogs help people? Can you name some professions for dogs?

6. Have you ever known an animal that rescued a person? How?

7. What's the most extraordinary thing you've heard a pet do?

8. What are some disadvantages to having pets? How could pets cause trouble?

9. Have you ever taken a pet to a veterinarian? Did it get a vaccination? Why?

REMEMBER...

Be active

Be open

Be sympathetic

10. Why do some cities encourage people to spay or neuter their pets?

11. How did you express your grief when your pet died? What did you do to honor your memories together?

12. Are pets treated different in the United States than your native country? Can you give an example?

13. Have you ever watched a dog show? What was your reaction?

14. Are you allergic to any animals? Which ones? What do you do for your allergies?

15. Can you name movies that star dogs? Other animals? Which was your favorite?

16. What books or songs celebrate dogs? Other pets? Which was your favorite?

17. What do you think children learn from having pets?

18. Pet robots and virtual pets are now available. Why do you think these hi-tech toys have become fashionable?

19. Who do you think might buy pet robots? Why?

20. Why are we so devoted to our pets? Why do we love them so much?

QUOTATIONS

Pick your favorite three quotations. Explain your choices.

1. "If you lie down with dogs, you'll rise up with fleas."
   —Benjamin Franklin (1706–1790), American icon

2. "Mad dogs and Englishmen go out in the noonday sun."
   —Noel Coward (1899–1973), dramatist

3. "A dog starved at his master's gate, Predicts the ruin of the state."
   —William Blake (1757–1827, English poet

4. "To his dog, every man is Napoleon; hence the popularity of dogs."
   —Aldous Huxley (1894–1963) British novelist

5. "The more I see of men, the more I like dogs."
   —Madame de Stael (1766–1817), French writer

6. "If you pick up a starving dog and make him prosperous, he will not bite you; that is the principal difference between a dog and a man."
   —Mark Twain (1835–1910), writer

7. "If man's best friend is a dog, his worst is dogma."
   —Leo Rosten (1908–1997), writer

8. "I like pigs. Dogs look up to us. Cat look down on us. Pigs treat us as equals."—Winston Churchill (1874–1965), British Prime Minister

9. "Animals are such agreeable friends–they ask no questions, they pass no criticisms."—George Elliot (1819–1890), English novelist

10. "What counts is not necessarily the size of the dog in the fight–it's the size of the fight in the dog."
    —Dwight D. "Ike" Eisenhower (1890–1969), 34th U.S. President

11. "Dogs are our link to paradise."
    —Milan Kundera (1929–) Franco-Czech novelist

ON YOUR OWN

Some people say that dogs and their owners look alike. As you walk or ride around in the next few days, observe dog owners and their dogs.

Try to find at least five examples. What do you think? Do dog owners resemble their dogs? What did you find out?

> "The way to keep a cat is
> to try and chase it away."
>
> Ed Howe (1853–1937),
> American humorist

12

CATS, AND MORE CATS

CHATTING

Pet owners often enjoy talking about their animals. Interview your partner.

1. Do you like cats? Are you a cat person? Why or why not?
2. Which do you like better, cats or dogs? Why?
3. Have you ever owned a cat? What was its name?
4. Do you prefer indoor cats or outdoor cats? Why?
5. How can cats be helpful to people?
6. Why do farmers often have cats in their barns?
7. What are some of the things that kittens like to play with?
8. How do cats keep clean? Have you ever tried to wash a cat?
9. Can you name a purebred long-haired cat?
10. Can you name a purebred short-haired cat?
11. Have you ever read the popular children's book *The Cat in the Hat*? Have you ever read any other books by Dr. Seuss?
12. Can you describe how a cat moves?
13. What are some colors that cats come in?
14. Can you make the purr sound a happy cat might make?
15. Can you make the hissing sound an angry cat might make?
16. Do you consider cats a blessing or a burden?
17. What is a feral cat? Are there many stray cats in your area?
18. Why do you think cats were considered sacred in ancient Egypt?
19. Can you name some of the big cats in the cat family?
20. Have you ever seen a lion or a tiger? Where?

VOCABULARY

Circle the words you know. Ask your partner about the other words.

kitten ....

sanctuary...

purr ....

circus ....

feral ....

hiss...

predator ....

roar...

endangered ....

stray..

NOTES & QUESTIONS

....

....

....

....

....

....

....

SENTENCES AND IDIOMS

What do these expressions mean? Discuss with your group.

Shh! Shh! Don't let the cat out of the bag.

Has the cat got your tongue?

She made a very catty remark about you.

He has the heart of a lion.

There's more than one way to skin a cat.

PROVERBS AND SAYINGS

Circle the proverbs that you have heard before. Add another.

A cat has nine lives.

While the cat's away, the mice will play.

Even a cat is a lion in her own lair.—Indian

When the mouse laughs at the cat,
there is a hole nearby.—Nigerian

Even the lion has to defend himself against flies.—German

THE CONVERSATION CONTINUES...

1. Do large cats like lions or jaguars roam wild in your native country?

2. Can you make the sound of a roar of a lion?

3. Why do you think a lion is called the "king of the jungle"? Which animal would you consider the peasant?

4. Have you ever hunted for a large cat? Would you like to? Why?

5. Have you seen large cats in zoos? Which zoos? Which cats?

6. Have you seen large cats in a circus? Which cats? What did they do?

7. Why do you think someone might become a lion tamer?

8. What is a predator? What animals are natural predators? Is man?

9. What are some ways that cats, big or small, are used as symbols?

10. What does "endangered" mean? What are some endangered animals?

11. Is it okay to kill endangered animals? Why or why not?

12. Can you think of anyone who had a lion, tiger, or other exotic animal as a pet?

13. Do you think a lion or tiger can really be a trustworthy pet?

14. What are animal sanctuaries? Why are they expanding?

15. What are some ways that people can help protect lions, panthers, and tigers?

16. What books, movies, paintings, etc. have been inspired by cats?

17. Why do both wild cats and domesticated pets fascinate humans?

QUOTATIONS

Pick your three favorite quotations. Memorize one of the three.

1. "An oppressive government is more to be feared than a tiger."
   —Confucius (551–479 B.C.E.), China's most influential philosopher

2. "I was not a lion, but it fell to me to give the lion's roar."
   —Winston Churchill (1874–1965), British orator and prime minister

3. "I'm like a lion–I roar. If someone betrays me, I won't be a victim. I don't sulk. I get angry."
   —Lisa Marie Presley (1968–), daughter of Elvis Presley

4. "When a man wants to murder a tiger, he calls it sport; when a tiger wants to murder him, he calls it ferocity."
   —George Bernard Shaw (1856–1950), playwright

5. "Women and cats will do as they please, and men and dogs should relax and get used to the idea."
   —Robert A. Heinlein (1907–1988), science fiction writer

6. "Lettin' the cat outta the bag is a whole lot easier 'n puttin' it back in."—Will Rogers (1879–1935), American entertainer

7. "'I know a good game we could play,' said the cat. 'I know some new tricks,' said the Cat in a Hat."
   —Dr. Seuss (1904–1991), author of children's books

8. "The tigers of wrath are wiser than the horses of instruction."
   —William Blake (1757–1827), English poet and artist

9. "One of the striking differences between a cat and a lie is that a cat has only nine lives."
   —Mark Twain (1835–1910), American writer and humorist

10. "With cats, some say, one rule is true: Don't speak till you are spoken to."—T.S. Eliot (1888–1965), British poet

ON YOUR OWN

In the Word Search, find and circle the following 10 words: KITTENS, TABBY, ROAR, LION, CLAW, TIGER, SIAMESE, MEOW, CAT, and MEW. The words may be across, up and down, or diagonal.

K	L	C	C	L	A	W
S	I	A	M	E	S	E
R	O	T	A	B	B	Y
O	N	I	T	M	Z	K
A	S	G	W	E	C	W
R	M	E	W	O	N	R
X	B	R	I	W	A	S

13
PET PEEVES

SHARING COMPLAINTS

Sometimes things annoy us, and that's okay. Share your complaints and pet peeves with your partner. Laughing and sighing can help.

1. What annoys you? Do you have any pet peeves?

2. Do you prefer sales pitches in person, by phone, or on TV? Why?

3. How can salespeople be annoying? Can you give some examples?

4. Have you ever had serious email problems? How did you respond?

5. What technology or gadget bothers you? Why?

6. Do you quickly figure out how new appliances work?

7. What common behavior do you often find offensive? Why?

8. What are some things that you find impolite? Give examples.

9. What is litter? Have you seen any litterbugs? Where does litter bother you most?

10. What do you consider bad cell phone manners or habits?

11. When, or where, do you most often see people stressed?

12. What behavior might be considered irritating in a neighbor? Have you ever had a noisy neighbor? Can you give an example of a difficult neighbor?

13. Is there a difference between assertive and aggressive? How do aggressive people make you feel? How do you tend to respond?

14. Are there many aggressive drivers in your area? Is "road rage" a problem?

15. What behavior would be strange for a man, but normal for a woman?

16. What behavior might seem odd for a woman, but normal for a man?

17. Is there a double standard for men and women? How? Is this fair?

VOCABULARY

Please circle the words that you know. Use them to write three questions.

annoy ....

rage ....

peeve ....

bother...

polite ....

impolite..

offended ....

courtesy..

litter..

litterbug..

obnoxious...

toxic..

profanity..

PROVERBS

Read the common sayings and proverbs below. Can you add two more?

Recite "patience" three times and it will spare you a murder.—Korean

This is done and I'm to blame
Therefore, know that I'm in shame.—Persian

Control yourself: remember anger
is only one letter short of danger.—School poster

Love makes a good eye squint.—English

The reputation of a thousand years may be
determined by the conduct of one hour.—Japanese

THE CONVERSATION CONTINUES...

1. What table manners or eating styles make you frown or annoy you?

2. When, if ever, does snoring, sneezing, or coughing bother you?

3. Where do you find adults generally act their worst? Why?

4. How does a polite child act? How does a rude child behave?

5. Where do people learn good manners? What are good manners?

6. What do you dislike about living here?

7. Can you describe a polite boss? A very difficult boss?

8. How have co-workers annoyed you? What did they do?
   How did you handle difficult co-workers?

9. How have you handled working with rude customers? Are you able
   to keep your cool?

10. Does foul language, or profanity, upset you? When?

11. What obnoxious ads have you had a strong negative reaction to?

REMEMBER...

Be yourself

Be honest

Make good mistakes

12. Have you ever walked out of a movie? Were you bored or offended? Why?

13. Are there personality traits that you find extremely disagreeable?

14. How can someone really make you "blow your lid" or explode? What brings out the worst in you? A family relative? A good friend?

15. What is something that once annoyed you that you have, over time, come to tolerate?

16. Have you seen any changes in what are considered good manners in your life? What?

17. Do you have any advice for dealing with difficult, moody, or "toxic" people?

QUOTATIONS

Read aloud all the quotations. Pick your favorites and discuss.

1. "If you empty a cup of wine in one gulp, you are a drunkard."
   —Talmud

2. "The test of good manners is to be patient with bad ones."
   —Solomon ibn Gabriol (1021–1051) Hebrew poet

3. "Good manners are made up of petty sacrifices."
   —Ralph Waldo Emerson (1803–1882), writer

4. "Be polite; write diplomatically; even in a declaration of war one observes the rules of politeness."
   —Otto von Bismarck (1815–1898), German Chancellor

5. "Never treat a guest like a member of the family—treat him with courtesy."
   —Evan Esar (1899–1935), American humorist

6. "My dad was the town drunk. Usually that's not so bad, but New York City?"—Henry Youngman, comedian

7. "Isn't it monstrous the way people go about saying things behind other people's backs that are absolutely and entirely true?"
   —Oscar Wilde (1854–1900), playwright

8. "In the first place, God made idiots; this was for practice. Then he made school boards."
   —Mark Twain (1835–1910), humorist

9. "The best way to be successful in Hollywood is to be as obnoxious as the next guy."
   —Sylvester Stallone (1946–), actor and director

10. "Being a star has made it possible for me to get insulted in places where the average Negro could never hope to get insulted."
    —Sammy Davis, Jr (1925–1990), American entertainer

11. "When you're down and out, something always turns up–usually the noses of your friends."
    —Orson Welles (1915–1985), actor and director

12. "Earthquakes bring out the worst in some guys."
    —George Kennedy in *Earthquake*

ON YOUR OWN

Give a one-minute presentation to the class on your biggest pet peeve.

Free Time

"Half our life is spent trying to find something to do with the time we have rushed through life trying to save."

WILL ROGERS
(1879–1935), comedian

TRAVELING

SHARING EXPERIENCES

Traveling can be wonderful or awful. How have you fared? Chat with your class partner about your travels.

1. What is your native country?

2. In which region or city did you live in your homeland?

3. Were there any nearby tourist attractions? If so, what were they?

4. What did you travel to see in your native land?

5. What spot in your homeland was most interesting to you? Why?

6. Would you recommend that tourists from other lands visit there? Why? Why not?

7. Are there popular vacation sites in your homeland? What are they?

8. Do you like to use travel guidebooks? Which ones? How are guidebooks useful?

9. What are some other good sources of travel information?

10. In which other countries have you traveled?

11. Did you plan where you would go before you left?

12. Did you make reservations ahead of time?

13. Did you travel alone or with others?

14. Of the places you have been, which was the prettiest?

15. Of the places you have been, which was the most impressive?

16. Of the places you have been, which was the most educational? How?

17. In the countries you visited, which people were the friendliest?

18. In the countries you visited, which people were the least friendly?

19. What languages have you spoken while traveling?

20. What are some useful phrases to learn in a foreign language? Why?

VOCABULARY

With the help if your partner, define the meaning of each of the following words or phrases.

site ....

homeland ....

native country ....

region ....

popular ....

recommend ....

luggage ....

eventually ....

cheated ....

exchanged ....

wander ....

impressive ....

PROVERBS

Can you add another proverb about traveling?

When in Rome, do as the Romans.—Latin

All roads lead to Rome.—Latin

Every land has its own law.—Scottish

Fish and visitors smell after three days.—American

In an undeveloped country, don't drink the water.
In a developed country, don't breathe the air.—Anonymous

Let yourself go.—Travel slogan

(Add your own) ....

THE CONVERSATION CONTINUES...

1. While traveling, were you ever afraid? Why?

2. While traveling, were you ever lost? Where were you?

3. Have you ever taken a tour? When? Where?

4. Have you ever asked a person on the street for help while you were traveling? What happened?

5. Have you ever asked for help from an embassy or Traveler's Aid?

5. What happened? Did you receive help?

6. Were you ever cheated by a store or restaurant while you were traveling? What did you say or do? How did you react?

7. Have you ever taken a wild taxi ride? What happened?

8. Did you ever lose your luggage? Did you eventually get it?

9. Where do you exchange money when you travel?
Is foreign money confusing?

REMEMBER...

Be curious

Be open

Have fun

10. Is there any country you would like to visit again? What sites would you visit?

11. Is there any country outside your native country in which you would like to live?

12. Where have you traveled in the United States?

13. Has any place surprised you? How was it different from what you expected?

14. Where would you like to travel next? Why? What would you most like to see?

QUOTATIONS

Read aloud each of the following quotations. Talk about their meaning with your partner. Then, circle your favorite.

1. "The world is a book, and those who do not travel read only a page."—Saint Augustine (354–430), Catholic theologian

2. "Your land and home and pleasant wife must be left behind." —Horace (65–8 B.C.E.), Roman lyric poet

3. "I travel for travel's sake." —Robert Louis Stevenson (1850–1894), writer

4. "What was important then was not that the beggar was drunk and reeling, but that he was mounted on his horse, and, however unsteadily, was going somewhere." —Thomas Wolfe in You Can't Go Home Again

5. "When traveling with someone, take large doses of patience and tolerance with your morning coffee." —Helen Hayes, (1900–1993), American actress

6. "He travels best who knows when to return." —Thomas Middleton (1580–1627), playwright

7. "What gives value to travel is fear."—Albert Camus (1913–1960), French writer, Nobel Prize for Literature

8. "Traveling is a fool's paradise." —Ralph Waldo Emerson (1803–1882), writer

9. "There is wisdom in turning as often as possible from the familiar to the unfamiliar; it keeps the mind nimble; it kills prejudice, and it fosters humor."—George Santayanya (1863–1952), philosopher

10. "…traveling, we are born again, able to return at moments to a younger and more open self." —Pico Iyer (1957–) travel writer

11. "Never go on trips with anyone you do not love." —Ernest Hemingway (1899–1961), Nobel Prize-winning novelist

12. "Travel is the best way we have of rescuing the humanity of places, and saving them from abstraction and ideology." —Pico Iyer (1957–) travel writer

13. "The traveler sees what he sees; the tourist sees what he has come to see."—G.K. Chesterton (1874–1936), English writer

ON YOUR OWN

Write a short report on a place you have been. Then, present your report to the class.

Use at least one map, photograph, or other visual aid so the class can more easily share your experience.

15
CALIFORNIA CALLING

CHATTING

California, nicknamed the Golden State, evokes many images. Americans have also created many myths about California with colorful posters, television shows, and numerous movies. Interview your partner and share your impressions of California.

1. What are some famous places in California?

2. What are some beautiful places in California?

3. Have you seen any pictures from California? What was in the picture?

4. Has California been in the news lately? Why?

5. Have you seen any movies that took place in California? Which?

6. Have you ever visited California? Why? When?

7. Have you ever lived in California? Where? When?

8. Can you name some cities in California?

9. Can you name any national parks in California?

10. Who are some famous people who have called California home?

11. How would you describe the climate in California?

12. How do you think being so close to Mexico has influenced California?

13. What are some cultural institutions in Los Angeles?

14. What are some tourist sights in San Francisco?

15. Which cities would you like to visit?

16. Where else would you like to visit in California? Why?

17. Do you have relatives in California? Who?

18. How would you prepare for a two-week trip to California?

19. Which adjectives would you use to describe California? Why?

20. Do you think you would like to live in California? Why?

VOCABULARY

With your partner, give short definitions for these words.

landscape ....

vacation...

memorable ....

gold rush ....

homesick ....

factors...

tipping point ....

distinctive ....

desert...

guidebook ....

nickname ....

attraction...

SAYINGS

Go West, young man.

As California goes, so goes America.

California is the America of America.

California is full of nuts and berries.

Hooray for Hollywood!

I left my heart in San Francisco.

THE CONVERSATION CONTINUES...

The California myth remains strong as over 35 million people pursue their American dreams in the nation's most populous state. Millions more have visited, and collected memories. These questions focus on their experiences in the Golden State.

1. What brought you to California? Business? Pleasure? Other?

2. How long did you spend in California?

3. Where did you enter California? Were you traveling alone?

4. Have you visited San Diego? Los Angeles? San Francisco?

5. Have you driven on the highways? Where did you go?

6. Do you like deserts? Have you been to Joshua Tree? Death Valley?

7. What adjectives do you think best describe Los Angeles? Why?

8. Have you visited a theme park? Disneyland? Universal Studios?

9. What made a strong first impression on you?

10. What surprised you about California? Why?

11. What are some advantages to living in California? Why?

12. What are some problems that face California residents?

13. What tips would you give a friend moving to California? Why?

14. Do you think California represents the American Dream? How?

QUOTATIONS

Read the quotations aloud, circle your favorites, and discuss at least one of them.

1. "Nowhere on the continent did Americans find a more diverse nature, a land of more impressive forms and more powerful contrasts, than in California."
   —Wallace Stegner (1909–1993), Western novelist

2. "The attraction and superiority of California are in its days. It has better days and more of them than any other country."
   —Ralph Waldo Emerson (1803–1882), American philosopher

3. "The first treasure California began to surrender after the Gold Rush was the oldest: her land."
   —John Jakes (1932–), novelist

4. "When I am in California, I am not in the west, I am west of the west."
   —Theodore Roosevelt (1858–1919), 26th U.S. President

5. "This land is your land, this land is my land, From California to the New York island, From the redwood forest to the Gulf Stream waters, This land was made for you and me."
   —Woody Guthrie (1912–1967), American folksinger

6. "It's a scientific fact that if you stay in California, you lose one point of IQ every year."
   —Truman Capote (1924–1984), writer

7. "San Francisco has only one drawback. 'Tis hard to leave."
   —Rudyard Kipling (1865–1936), British novelist

8. "The coldest winter I ever spent was a summer in San Francisco."
   —Mark Twain (1835–1910), humorist and novelist

9. "Tip the world over on its side and everything loose will land in Los Angeles."
   —Frank Lloyd Wright (1867–1959), architect

10. "There is science, logic, reason; there is thought verified by experience. And then there is California."
    —Edward Abbey (1927–1989), environmentalist

11. "California is a tragic country…like every Promised Land."
    —Christopher Isherwood (1904–1986), dramatist and author

12. "Whatever starts in California, unfortunately, has an inclination to spread"
    —Jimmy Carter (1924–), 39th U.S. President

13. "We have to get back and bring California back to where it once was."
    —Arnold Schwarzenegger (1947–), 38th California Governor and actor

14. "California has become the first American state where there is no majority race, and we're doing just fine. If you look around the room, you can see a microcosm of what we can do in the world."
    —Bill Clinton (1946–), 42nd U.S. President

ON YOUR OWN

Where do you want to go in California?

Research a tourist destination, museum, or city in California Check websites, talk to people who know the place, and look at pictures.

Prepare a short oral report for the class. Use visual aids.

16
READING PLEASURES AND TASTES

EXCHANGING VIEWS

Reading is a solitary activity, yet it can bring people together in conversation. Interview your partner and exchange reading experiences.

1. Have you ever re-read a book? Which? Why? How many times?

2. Do you have a library card yet? Do you like to browse in bookstores?

3. What book, or author, has influenced you the most? How?

4. Have you ever been in a book club? Did your club focus on a genre?

5. Did your mother read to you as a child? Did you have a favorite story? What was it?

6. Did you have a favorite book character as a child?

7. Where did you first learn to read? At home? School? Church?

8. What language did you first learn to read in?

9. What were your favorite books as a child? Who was your favorite author? Why?

10. What kind of books does your mother read? Your father? Your children? Your siblings?

11. What did you like to read in high school? Why?

12. What was your favorite book that you had to read in school?

13. What was your least favorite book that you were assigned to read? Why?

14. As a teenager, did you have any favorite books, comics, or magazines? Can you describe them?

15. Do you read emails? Postcards? Websites? Blogs? Newspapers? Magazines?

16. Which magazine or newspaper sections do you scan? Why?

17. Who are some famous writers from your country?

18. Who are some famous writers who write in your native language?

VOCABULARY

Circle the words that you know. Then write a long sentence using at least three of these vocabulary words. Share your sentence with your partner.

literature..

browse...

genre...

essays...

novels..

memoir..

re-read..

poem...

poet...

biography..

autobiography..

scan...

PROVERBS

What experiences might have inspired these proverbs?

Drink nothing without seeing it;
sign nothing without reading it.—Spanish

When all else fails, read the instructions.

You can't tell a book by its cover.

So many books, so little time.

Reading is addictive.

THE CONVERSATION CONTINUES...

1. Can you think of some movies that are adapted from novels?

2. Can you suggest a good movie that was originally a book? Can you compare the movie or the book?

3. Do you prefer to read poems, essays, or short stories? Why?

4. Do you prefer reading fiction or non-fiction? Why?

5. Do you have a favorite poet or short story writer? Who?

6. Did you have to memorize any poems in school? Which?

7. Have you ever listened to an audio book? Which one? Why?

8. Where do you find books? Have you bought any books online?

9. Have you read any good biographies? Memoirs? Self-help books?

10. What are some books that you have read and enjoyed?

11. What kinds of books do you tend to read? Dislike? Why?

12. Why do you think book clubs have become so popular in the U.S.?

13. How do you select books? Covers? Ads? Book reviews? Word of mouth? Gifts?

REMEMBER...

Be curious

Explore

Be tolerant

14. What magazines do you read? Which articles attract you? Why?

15. Are you reading a book now? What is it? Can you describe it?

16. What do your friends and relatives like to read?

17. Do you think books and magazines make good gifts? Why?

18. Have you read any controversial or banned books?

19. What book are you planning to read in English this year? Why?

QUOTATIONS

Memorize your favorite quotation and author's name. Share it with someone.

1. "Reading is to the mind what exercise is to the body."
   —Richard Steele (1672–1729), Irish writer

2. "No entertainment is so cheap as reading, nor any pleasure so lasting."
   —Lady Mary Wortley Montagu (1689–1762), British author/critic

3. "The pleasure of all reading is doubled when one lives with another who shares the same books."
   —Katherine Mansfield (1888–1923), short story writer and poet

4. "However many holy words you read, however many you speak, what good will they do you if you do not act upon them?"
   —Buddha (563–483 B.C.E.), founder of Buddhism

5. "Read the best books first, or you may not have a chance to read them at all."
   —Henry David Thoreau (1817–1862), essayist

6. "Some books are to be tasted, others to be swallowed, and some few to be chewed and digested."
   —Sir Francis Bacon (1561–1626), English essayist

7. "I would rather be poor in a cottage full of books than a king without the desire to read."
   —Thomas B. Macaulay (1800–1859), historian

8. "This is not a novel to be tossed aside lightly. It should be thrown with great force."
   —Dorothy Parker (1893–1967), screenwriter

9. "A book should serve as the ax for the frozen sea within us."
   —Franz Kafka (1883–1924), novelist

10. "There is a great deal of difference between the eager man who wants to read a book and the tired man who wants a book to read."
    —G.K. Chesterton (1874–1936), novelist

11. "A home without books is like a body without a soul."
    —Cicero (106–43 B.C.E.), statesman

12. "Any book that helps a child to form the habit of reading, to make reading one of his deep and continuing needs, is good for him."
    —Maya Angelou (1928–), American poet

13. "Where they burn books, they will end in burning human beings."
    —Heinrich Heine (1797–1856), German poet

ON YOUR OWN

Bring in a book which is important to you. Show the book to the class. Tell them the author, the title, and the reason why this book is important to you.

17

MOVING TO MUSIC

SHARING MUSICAL MOMENTS

Music is a universal language. Compare your music taste with that of others in groups of three or four classmates.

1. What kinds of music do you like?

2. What is one of your favorite songs?

3. Where do you like to be when you listen to music?

4. Do you like to sing? What is your favorite song to sing?

5. Can you carry a tune? Are you tone deaf?

6. Can you name some popular musicals?

7. Can you name a song from a musical? Can you sing or hum a song from a musical?

8. Have you ever sung in public? Have you ever been in a choir? Where?

9. Is your voice soprano, alto, tenor, or bass?

10. Do you like to sing to yourself? Where?

11. Have you ever been to a karaoke bar? Did you sing? Which songs?

12. What kind of music is traditionally popular in your native country?

13. Which instruments are used to play this traditional music?

14. Which kinds of American music do you like?

15. Do you like rap? Can you name a rap star?

16. Do you like salsa? Bosa nova? The tango?

17. What kind of music do you dance to?

18. Do you like jazz? Who is your favorite jazz musician?

19. Which are your favorite groups? Which groups did you like as a teenager?

20. Who are your favorite singers? How do they make you feel?

VOCABULARY

Circle the words you know. Find the meaning of the others with your classroom partner.

tone deaf ....

salsa ....

musician ....

yearn ....

symphony ....

vocalist ....

opera ....

concert ....

downloaded ....

instrument ....

compose ....

composer ....

THE CONVERSATION CONTINUES...

1. Have you ever been to a concert? Who did you see? What did you hear? Did you find it satisfying?

2. If you won free tickets from a radio station, which group or vocalist would you like to see in concert? Why?

3. Have you ever taken piano lessons or lessons on any musical instrument? Which one? How long did you take lessons?

4. Did you ever play in a band? Was it a marching band?

5. Do you like classical music? Who are some significant composers of classical music?

6. Have you ever been to a symphony? What was it like?

7. Can you name some operas? Can you name some opera stars?

8. How do you find new music? Radio? MTV? Internet?

9. Have you ever downloaded music? What kind of music?

10. Can you recommend websites to help find great new music?

11. Do you have a favorite music video? Musical?

12. Do you have any soundtracks from movies? Which ones?

13. What music did you play at your wedding or wedding reception?

14. Are there any songs you've heard which made you want to travel to a particular place? Which songs? Where did you yearn to go?

15. Can you suggest some places to hear live music? Is there a cover charge?

16. If you could have a date with a musician, whom would you choose?

17. If you were trapped on a desert island and could only take five albums with you, which would you pick? Why?

Read aloud all the quotations. Pick your favorites and discuss.

1. "Virtue is the trunk of man's nature, and music is the blossoming of virtue."
   —Confucius (551–479 B.C.E.), legendary social philosopher

2. "Music I heard with you was more than music. Bread I broke with you was more than bread."
   —Conrad Aiken (1889–1973), American poet and novelist

3. "Music is love in search of a word."
   —Sidney Lanier (1842–1881), poet

4. "Music hath charms to soothe the savage beast
   To soften rocks, or bend a knotted oak."
   —William Congreve (1670–1729), English playwright

5. "Without music, life would be a mistake."
   —Friedrich Nietzsche (1844–1900), writer

6. "Even if you can't sing well, sing. Sing to yourself. Sing in the privacy of your home. But sing."
   —Rabbi Nachman of Breslov (1772–1810), religious leader

7. "God respects me when I work, but he loves me when I sing."
   —Rabindranath Tagore (1861–1941) Indian poet and musician

8. "Musical people always want one to be perfectly dumb at the very moment when one is longing to be absolutely deaf."
   —Oscar Wilde (1856–1900), playwright

9. "If a man does not keep pace with his companions, perhaps it is because he hears a different drummer. Let him step to the music which he hears, however measured or far away."
   —Henry David Thoreau (1817–1862), American writer

10. "Unperformed music is like a cake in the oven–not fully baked."
    —Isaac Stern (1920–), Russian violinist

11. "My music is best understood by children and animals."
    —Igor Stravinsky (1882–1971), Russian composer

12. "It is impossible to experience one's own death objectively and still carry a tune."
    —Woody Allen (1935–), American film director and comedian

13. "After silence, that which comes nearest to expressing the inexpressible is music."
    —Aldous Huxley (1894–1963), English novelist

14. "Music melts all the separate parts of our bodies together."
    —Anaïs Nin (1903–1977), French-American author

15. "When you play music you discover a part of yourself that you never knew existed."
    —Bill Evans (1829–1980), American jazz pianist

ON YOUR OWN

Research a favorite musician, composer, instrument, or piece of music. Write a short paragraph about your chosen subject and read it to a small group.

18

TALKING ABOUT TELEVISION

GETTING ACQUAINTED

Almost everybody watches television, but somehow many people feel ashamed of doing it. Interview your partner and find out about their tastes in TV shows.

1. When did you start watching TV? How many years have you watched television?

2. Were the TV shows in color or black and white?

3. When did your family first get a television? Why?

4. Did you have some favorite TV shows, cartoons, or characters as a child? Why?

5. Where did you do you usually watch TV? With whom did you watch?

6. Did you ever watch any English language programs as a child?

7. How many television sets are in your home today? Which do you use the most?

8. How many channels do you receive at home? How many do you regularly watch?

9. What television programs do you like to watch with your family?

10. What TV programs do you like to watch with your friends? Alone?

11. Do you eat while watching television? Pay bills? Wash dishes? Knit? Quilt? Do crafts?

12. What are your favorite television programs now? Why?

13. Do you pay for cable or satellite? Do you subscribe to any channels like HBO?

14. Do you follow any dramatic series on a regular basis? Which?

15. How many hours, on a weekly basis, do you usually watch?

16. Would you like to watch more television? What would you like to watch more?

17. Do you ever feel guilty about watching television? Why?

VOCABULARY

Circle the words that you know. Write questions using new words.

series...

drama...

crime..

channels..

subscribe ....

cater ....

broadcast...

personalities..

reality TV ....

characters...

controversy...

closed-captioned ....

THE CONVERSATION CONTINUES...

1. When are you most likely to watch television? Where? Why?

2. When are you least likely to watch television? Where? Why?

3. Are there more channels than when you were a child? Can you give an example?

4. What are some influential television programs in your country?

5. What television programs can you recommend for children? Young adults? Why?

6. Can you suggest some programs for seniors? Why?

7. What languages are programs broadcast in your city? Which channels seem to cater to immigrant populations?

8. Do you watch programs closed-captioned (for the deaf) or subtitled?

9. Do you find American TV shows educational? Strange? Funny? Why? Can you give an example?

10. Have you seen any reality TV shows? Which? What did you think?

11. What are some popular crime and detective shows? Which? Why?

12. Who are some famous TV personalities or stars? Any personal favorites?

13. Who is Oprah? Jerry Springer? Larry King? Jon Stewart? Homer Simpson?

14. What TV shows would you recommend to a visitor to the United States? Why?

15. Have you found any differences between the TV news coverage in your country and the United States? Can you give an example?

16. How has television changed in the last decade? How would you like to change TV?

17. What do you think are some social effects of television? Why?

REMEMBER...

Be curious

Explore

Have fun

Read the quotations aloud with your partner. Pick four to discuss.

1. "Television could perform a great service in mass education, but there's no indication its sponsors have anything like this on their minds."—Tallulah Bankhead (1903–1968), American actress

2. "I find television very educating. Every time somebody turns on the set, I go into the other room and read a book."
—Groucho Marx (1890–1977), comedian

3. "In the age of television, image becomes more important than substance."
—S.I. Hayakawa (1906–1992), U.S. Senator from California

4. "Television is an invention that permits you to be entertained in your living room by people you wouldn't have in your home."
—David Frost (1939–), British broadcast journalist

5. "Television is the first truly democratic culture—the first culture available to everybody and entirely governed by what the people want. The most terrifying thing is what people want."
—Clive Barnes (1927–), critic and author

6. "Seeing a murder on television can help work off one's antagonisms. And if you haven't any antagonisms, the commercials will give you some."—Alfred Hitchcock (1899–1980), British film director

7. "When television is good, nothing is better. When it's bad, nothing is worse."—Newton N. Minow (1926–), media critic

8. "Television is not real life. In real life, people actually have to leave the coffee shop and go to jobs."
—Bill Gates (1955–), American entrepreneur and philanthropist

9. "Television has proved that people will look at anything rather than each other."—Ann Landers (1918–2002), advice columnist

10. "I want to use television not only to entertain, but to help people lead better lives."
—Oprah Winfrey (1954–) TV host, producer, and actress

11. "Television! Teacher, mother, secret lover."
—Homer Simpson, cartoon character

12. "I hate television. I hate it as much as peanuts. But I can't stop eating peanuts."—Orson Welles (1915–1985) American actor

13. "Television is a method to deliver advertising like a cigarette is a method to deliver nicotine."—Bill Maher (1956–) social critic

14. "Television, that insidious beast, that Medusa which freezes a billion people to stone every night, staring fixedly, that siren which called and sang and promised so much and gave, after all, so little."
—Ray Bradbury (1920–) American science fiction writer

15. "Television brought the brutality of the war into the comfort of the living room. Vietnam was lost in the living rooms of America—not on the battlefields of Vietnam."
—Marshall McLuhan (1911–1980) media scholar

16. "Life doesn't imitate art; it imitates bad television."
—Woody Allen (1935–) comedian

ON YOUR OWN

Please complete this sentence: I would like to be on the TV show

....

because...

....

19

TALKING ABOUT MOVIES

CHATTING

You can also start a conversation by asking for movie suggestions. Talk with your partner, and share your movie experiences.

1. Do you like movies? Where do you usually see movies?

2. How often do you watch movies? At home? In theatres?

3. Where do you find movies to watch at home? Library? Cable? Blockbuster? Netflix?

4. Do you have cable television? Do you use on-demand features?

5. Do you own any movies? Which? Do you repeatedly watch them?

6. Have you figured out a way to see movies for free? How?

7. Can you compare movie houses in your homeland with theatres in the United States?

8. What might annoy you at a movie theatre? Using phones? Babies crying? Other?

9. Do you have a favorite movie theatre? A preferred place to sit?

10. Have you ever seen a celebrity or famous person? Where? Tell us about it

11. What movies have been blockbusters here? In your native country?

12. Can you think of some tourist sights related to the movie industry?

13. What movies have you seen that took place in Los Angeles? New York? Chicago?

14. Have you ever seen movies being filmed? Where? What was the atmosphere?

15. Have you ever acted in a play or movie? Can you describe your experience?

GENRES

Adventure

Animation

Biography

Comedy

Detective

Documentary

Drama

Fantasy

Film Noir

Foreign

Historical

Horror

Musical

Mystery

Propaganda

Romantic

Science Fiction

Silent

War

Western

VOCABULARY

With your partner, write definitions for five vocabulary words.

blockbuster..

famous..

popular..

adapt..

word of mouth ....

cast ....

crush...

celebrity ....

director..

genre ....

film noir ....

animation...

MOVIE GENRES

1. Which types (genres) of movies do you enjoy most? Why?

2. Can you think of an example of a good movie in five different categories?

3. Can you think of an example of a bad movie in three categories?

4. What makes your favorite films special or memorable?

5. Name a few movies that you disliked. Why did you dislike them?

6. Can you think of some books that have been adapted into movies? Did the adaptations work?

7. Did you have a favorite movie as a child? Teenager?

8. Did you have a favorite star as a child or teenager? Who? Why?

9. Do you know anybody who had a "crush" on a famous actor or actress?

10. Have you ever seen a movie several times? Which? Why?

11. Do you have any favorite actors now? Why? Did they move you in any role?

12. What actors, actresses, or directors would you like to lunch with?

13. Do you have any favorite directors? Why? Which of that director's films touched you?

14. How do you decide which movie to see? Word of mouth? Ads? Awards? Reviews?

15. Which movies would you suggest a tourist to your country watch? Why?

16. What movies have you seen this year? Which do you recommend?

17. Do you think movies influence society or reflect society? How?

Circle four quotes that appeal to you. Discuss your choices.

1. "Movies are a fad. Audiences really want to see live actors on a stage."
   —Charlie Chaplin (1889–1977), British comedian and actor

2. "You know what your problem is? It's that you haven't seen enough movies—all of life's riddles are answered in the movies."
   —Steve Martin (1945–), comedian

3. "I think nudity on screen is disgusting, shameful, and unpatriotic. But if I were twenty-two, with a great body, it would be artistic, tasteful, patriotic, and a progressive, religious experience."
   —Shelly Winters (1920–2006), actress

4. "Watch this if you like, and if you don't, take a hike."
   —Clint Eastwood (1930–), actor, director, and producer

5. "It's the movies that have really been running things in America ever since they were invented. They show you what to do, how to do it, when to do it, how to feel about it, and how to look how you feel about it."
   —Andy Warhol (1928–1987), American artist

6. "We need families to start taking more responsibility in understanding which movie is good for their children and which movie is not."
   —Jet Li (1963–), Chinese actor and martial artist

7. "Movies are fun, but they're not a cure for cancer."
   —Warren Beatty (1937–), American actor, director, and producer

8. "I did a women's movie, and I'm not a woman. I did a gay movie, and I'm not gay. I learned as I went along."
   —Ang Lee (1954–), film director born in Taiwan

9. "My movies were the kind they show in prisons and airplanes because nobody can leave."
   —Burt Reynolds (1936–), American actor

10. "Acting is not an important job in the scheme of things. Plumbing is."
    —Spencer Tracy (1900–1967), actor

11. "Maybe every other American movie shouldn't be based on a comic book."
    —Bill Maher (1956–), American comedian

12. "Life is like a movie, write your own ending. Keep believing, keep pretending."
    —Jim Henson (1936–1990), American creator of the Muppets

13. "The difference between life and the movies is that a script has to make sense, and life doesn't."
    —Joseph L. Mankiewicz (1909–1993), American screenwriter

ON YOUR OWN

Tell your classmates which movie you think should get a special Oscar for being the best movie ever made.

20

TALKING ABOUT MOVIES: THE SEQUEL

REVIEWING MOVIES

Once is not always enough. But can lightning strike a second time? Discuss movie remakes and sequels with your partner.

1. Can you think of any hit movies that led to a sequel?

2. Can you think of any remakes of classic films?

3. What's the difference between a remake and a sequel?

4. Can you think of a series of movies besides *Star Wars* and *Batman*?

5. Are you a fan of the *Spiderman* series? *Planet of the Apes*? Why?

6. Why do some films have two different versions?

7. What are some good movies based on good novels?

8. What are some bad movies based on good novels? What went wrong?

9. Do you enjoy movie previews? Why? Are any misleading? Exciting?

10. Do you like reading movie reviews? Why? Have you been misled?

11. Do you have any memories of seeing movies outdoors or at drive-in theatres? Where?

12. Have you ever walked out during previews? During a movie?

13. What are some job titles in the film industry?

14. Would you like to be an actor? Set designer? Extra? Make-up artist? Cinematographer? Stunt person? Costume designer?

15. What are some perks of working the film industry? Disadvantages?

16. Do you know any film snobs? What makes them film snobs?

17. What movie "wowed" you with special effects? Why?

18. Can you name some "chick flicks"? What makes a movie a "chick flick"? Do you like them?

19. What's the most exciting, or thrilling, movie you've seen? Why?

20. Can you name a Charlie Chaplin or Buster Keaton movie?

VOCABULARY

Read these words aloud.

sequel ....

remake ....

mislead ....

preview ....

review ....

wow ....

chick flick ....

thrill ....

soundtrack ....

shriek ....

snob ....

perk ....

Write four questions with using some of these words.

1. ....

2. ....

3. ....

4. ....

THE CONVERSATION CONTINUES...

1. Which silent movies have you seen? What was your take?

2. What are some movies with terrific costumes or set designs?

3. Have you ever cried in a movie? Why?

4. Do you laugh out loud during movies? Do you laugh easily?

5. What movies featured wonderful music or a great soundtrack?

6. What are some of the funniest films you've seen?

7. Why do you think scary movies, or horror films, remain popular?

8. Have you seen people hide their face during scary scenes? Jump? Scream? Do you do any of these actions?

9. What's the most disturbing scene you've seen in a movie? Why was it so memorable?

10. Do you watch the Academy Awards show? Why?

11. What's your partner's favorite film? Your children's favorite film?

12. Do you and your relatives have the same taste in movies?

13. What five movies would you take on a desert island?

REMEMBER...

Ask questions that seem natural

Be honest

Take risks

QUOTES FROM FAMOUS MOVIES

Pick your favorite. Explain your choice.

1. "Wait a minute, wait a minute. You ain't heard nothing yet."
   —Al Jolson in *The Jazz Singer* (1927)

2. "Toto, I've got a feeling we're not in Kansas any more."
   —Judy Garland in *The Wizard of Oz* (1939)

3. "Frankly, my dear, I don't give a damn."
   —Clark Gable in *Gone With the Wind* (1939)

4. "Play it, Sam. Play 'As Time Goes By'."
   —Humphrey Bogart in *Casablanca* (1942)

5. "You don't understand! I coulda had class. I coulda been a contender. I could've been somebody, instead of a bum, which is what I am."
   —Marlon Brando in *On the Waterfront* (1954)

6. "Gentleman, you can't fight in here! This is the War Room!"
   —Peter Sellers in *Dr. Strangelove* (1964)

7. "Mrs. Robinson, you're trying to seduce me. Aren't you?"
   —Dustin Hoffman in *The Graduate* (1967)

8. "I'm going to make him an offer he can't refuse."
   —Marlon Brando in *The Godfather* (1972)

9. "May the force be with you."
   —Alec Guinness in *Star Wars* (1977)

10. "Listen to me, mister. You're my knight in shining armor. Don't you forget it."
    —Katharine Hepburn in *On Golden Pond* (1981)

11. "Go ahead, make my day."
    —Clint Eastwood in *Sudden Impact* (1983)

12. "I'll be back."
    —Arnold Schwarzenegger in *The Terminator* (1984)

13. "Carpe Diem. Seize the day, boys. Make your lives extraordinary."
    —Robin Williams in *Dead Poets Society* (1989)

14. "Show me the money!"
    —Tom Cruise in *Jerry Maguire* (1996)

15. "I'm king of the world!"
    —Leonardo DiCaprio in *Titanic* (1997)

16. "Let's have some new clichés."
    —Samuel Goldwyn (1879–1974), producer

ON YOUR OWN

Tell your classmates which actor should receive a special Oscar for being the best movie actor of all time. For which role should he win this Oscar?

Tell your classmates which actress should receive a special Oscar for being the best movie actress of all time. For which role should she win this Oscar?

21

PLAYING AND WATCHING SPORTS

CHATTING

Talking about sports can be a great ice-breaker. Just do it!

1. Did you play any sports as a child? Which ones? Which was your favorite?

2. Do you play any sports? Which ones? Which sport is your favorite? Why?

3. Do girls and women play sports in your native country? If so, which sports are popular with females?

4. What is the most popular sport in your native country?

5. What equipment or uniform is needed for this sport?

6. How is the game scored? How is a tie decided? What is considered a high score?

7. How long is a game? Are there referees? How do fans usually behave? Are there cheerleaders?

8. Which athlete is best known in your homeland? Which sport does he or she play? What do people admire about this athlete?

9. Does your native country participate in the Olympics? In which sports are your countrymen most competitive?

10. What are some team sports? Which do you play?

11. What are some individual sports that you know? Which do you play?

12. Do you prefer to play team sports or individual sports? Why?

13. Which is your favorite sport to watch? Do watch any annual televised sporting event?

14. Have you ever gone to a sporting event? How did the fans behave?

15. Are you a fan of any special team? What do you like about them?

16. What is their nickname, e.g., Chicago Bulls, New England Patriots?

17. What does their nickname hope to convey about the team?

VOCABULARY

Do you know all these words? Can you add four more words to this list?

athlete ....

score ....

mascot ....

equipment ....

competition ....

referee ....

nickname ....

rival ....

endorse ....

endorsement ....

fan ....

brand ....

1. ....

2. ....

3. ....

4. ....

REMEMBER...

Be active

Just do it

Make good mistakes

THE CONVERSATION CONTINUES...

1. Does your favorite team have a main rival? Why?

2. Is there a team mascot?

3. Which American athletes are well known in your native land?

4. What are some of the ways that athletes train for competition?

5. What do you think is the difference between a game and a sport? Is chess a sport? Is weight lifting a sport? Is auto racing a sport? Is politics a sport?

6. Do you consider poker a game or a sport? Why?

7. Who is your favorite athlete? Why do you especially admire this athlete?

8. Do you buy a certain brand of shoes or clothes because of an athlete's endorsement? If so, which brand? Which athlete?

9. Can you name some sports that involve animals?

10. Is there any sport that you don't play now, but that you'd like to learn? Do you think you would do well?

11. Do you think any sport rules should be changed? Why?

12. If you could, would you outlaw any sports? Why?

13. Are there any sports which are legal in your homeland, but illegal in the U.S.? Why? Do you think these sports should be legal?

14. What are the differences between the way athletes are treated in your native country and the way athletes are treated in the U.S.?

15. Are there any disadvantages to playing sports? Examples?

16. What are some advantages to playing sports? How do you feel while playing?

17. If you could play against any athlete in any sport, what sport would you choose?

18. If you could go back in time and attend any sporting event, which would you pick? Why?

19. What makes a great athlete? Who do you think is the greatest athlete of our time? Why?

20. Do you think sports builds character? How?

21. Or do you believe sports reveals character?

IDIOMS

Try to guess the meanings of these idioms with your partner.

She's a team player. She knows the game plan.

The biology test was a slam dunk.

The price you're asking is in the ballpark.

When I caught Bob's finger in the car door, he was a good sport about it.

You dropped the ball.

QUOTATIONS

Which quotations do you like? Can you add one more?

1. "Sports do not build character. They reveal it."
   —Heywood Hale Broun (1888–1939), American sports journalist

2. "If you don't try to win, you might as well hold the Olympics in somebody's backyard."
   —Jesse Owens (1913–1980), American with four Olympic gold medals

3. "Sports is the toy department of human life."
   —Howard Cosell (1918–1995), sportscaster

4. "Sports is like a war without the killing."
   —Ted Turner (1938–), founder of CNN

5. "It ain't over till it's over."
   —Yogi Berra (1925–), American baseball coach

6. "Whoever wants to know the heart and mind of America had better learn baseball."
   —Jacques Barzun (1907–), American historian

7. "The less effort, the faster and more powerful you will be."
   —Bruce Lee (1940–1973), film star

8. "Golf is a good walk spoiled."
   —Mark Twain (1835–1910), humorist

9. "Aggressive fighting for the right is the noblest sport in the world."
   —Theodore Roosevelt (1859–1919), 26th U.S. President, sportsman

10. "…no boy from a rich family ever made the big leagues."
    —Joe DiMaggio (1914–), American baseball player

11. "Friendships born on the field of athletic strife are the real gold of competition. Awards become corroded, friends gather no dust."
    —Jesse Owens (1913–1980), four-time Gold medalist in 1936 Olympic Games

12. "If you're not cheating, you're not trying."
    —American sports proverb

13. "Good teams become great ones when the members trust each other enough to surrender the 'me' for the 'we.'"
    —Phil Jackson (1945–), L.A. Lakers' coach

14. "How can you think and hit at the same time?"
    —Yogi Berra (1925–), baseball player and coach

15. "There is no 'I' in team, but there is in 'win'."
    —Michael Jordan (1963–) NBA superstar

16. "Just do it."
    —Nike advertising slogan

ON YOUR OWN

Find a picture of an athlete, professional or amateur, playing your favorite sport. Cut it out, bring it to class, and describe the picture and its context.

22

GARDENING

SMALL TALK

You can always start a friendly conversation by complimenting neighbors on their gardens. Let's practice chatting about flowers, plants, and gardening now.

1. Do you like flowers? Which ones?

2. What is your favorite flower? Why? Can you describe it?

3. Which flowers have you ever given, or received, as a gift?

4. Can you describe a beautiful garden that you've seen?

5. Have you ever visited a famous or special garden? Where? When?

6. Have you ever nurtured a flower garden? Pruned a bush? Where?

7. What kinds of flowers were in your garden? Your home?

8. Do you grow flowers, herbs, fruits, or vegetables now? Which ones?

9. Are there others you would like to grow? Which ones?

10. What tasks do you enjoy doing in a garden?

11. What do you dislike about working in a garden?

12. What is a weed? Do gardeners need to weed a lot? Why?

13. Are there flowers that grow readily where you live now which are rare in your native country? Which ones? Why?

14. Are certain flowers associated with special occasions, like weddings, holidays, or funerals in your country of origin?

15. Have you ever visited a scent garden? Where? When?

16. What flowers and herbs might be found in a scent garden?

17. Do you usually use herbs when preparing traditional dishes? Which?

18. Have you ever heard of a plant being used to help cure an illness? Which plants? What were they used for?

19. Have you ever heard of plants being used to help one's love life? Which plants? Are there flowers traditionally given to lovers?

VOCABULARY

Please circle four words that you know, and create a question for each.

rare...

herb...

tasks...

plant...

weed...

scarce ....

scent ....

widespread...

export...

hobby ....

....

....

....

....

....

....

....

PROVERBS

Read the common sayings and proverbs below. Can you add two more?

He who plants a garden, plants happiness.—Chinese

As is the gardener, so is the garden.—Hebrew

The lotus springs from the mud.—Chinese

A garden is a thing of beauty and a job forever.—English

Sow soy beans, and you will reap soy beans;
sow red beans and you will reap red beans.—Korean

To plant a garden is to believe in tomorrow.

(Add your own) ....

(Add your own) ....

THE CONVERSATION CONTINUES...

1. Have you ever grown vegetables or fruits for your own use? When? Where?

2. Which vegetables or fruits did you have in your garden? Where did you get them?

3. What did you like about growing your own produce?

4. What did you dislike about cultivating vegetables and fruits?

5. What were "victory gardens" in World War II? How did they help win the war?

6. Does your native country export flowers, herbs, vegetables or fruits? Which?

7. What are some differences in climate between your native country and here?

8. Is water scarce in your native country? Is water expensive?

9. What are some drought resistant plants?

10. What are some famous gardens in the world today?

11. What are some of the differences in tools and work practices in gardens between what are commonly used in your country of origin and here?

12. What are some famous gardens from religion, history, and myth? Which would you most like to visit?

13. If you had unlimited money and were able to have the garden of your dreams, would you garden yourself or would you hire others to do it? Why?

14. What makes a good gardener? Which character traits might help?

15. How does gardening as a hobby help people develop a positive outlook?

QUOTATIONS

Circle a quotation that you like and memorize it.

1. "As you sow, so shall you reap."—Bible, Galatians

2. "We must cultivate our own garden."
   —Francois Voltaire (1694–1778), French writer

3. "People who think they can run the earth should begin with a small garden."—Evan Esar (1899–1995), humorist and columnist

4. "No occupation is so delightful to me as the culture of the earth and no culture comparable to that of the garden."
   —Thomas Jefferson (1743–1826), statesman, architect

5. "You can pick all the flowers, but you can not stop the spring."
   —Pablo Neruda (1904–1973), Chilean poet

6. "A weed is no more than a flower in disguise, Which is seen through at once, if love give a man eyes."
   —James Russell Lowell (1819–1891), American poet, diplomat

7. "I don't accept flowers. I take nothing perishable."
   —Paulette Goddard (1910–1990), actress

8. "A fool sees not the same tree that a wise man sees."
   —William Blake (1757–1827), English poet and painter

9. "If a tree dies, plant another in its place."
   —Carl Linnaeus (1707–1778), Swedish botanist

10. "The best place to find God is in a garden. You can dig for him there."—George Bernard Shaw (1856–1950), Irish playwright

11. "Life is not a puzzle to be solved, but a garden to be nurtured and enjoyed." —Toni Aberson (1937–) teacher and gardener

12. "When I go into my garden with a spade, and dig a bed, I feel such an exhilaration and health, that I discover that I have been defrauding myself all this time in letting others do for me what I should have done with my own hands."
    —Ralph Waldo Emerson (1803–1882), author and essayist

13. "If we could be understand a single flower we might know who we are and what the world is."
    —Jorge Luis Borges (1899–1986), Argentinian writer

ON YOUR OWN

Learn the English name for three flowers that you find pretty.

1. ....

2. ....

3. ....

23

ENJOYING THE BEACH

SHARING STORIES

Many people find a beach to be restful—a place for fun, relaxation, and renewal. Chat with your conversation partner about your beach experiences. Remember to be patient, cheerful, helpful, and encouraging.

1. How old were you when you first saw an ocean? Which ocean?

2. Have you ever taken a beach vacation? Where did you go?

3. Did you sunbath, jog, or read on the beach? Did you swim or wade in the waves?

4. When is your favorite time to be on the beach? Dawn, noon, or dusk? Why? What makes this time special at the beach?

5. What activities do you like to do at the beach?

6. Do you have any photographs of the beach?
   Can you describe a favorite one?

7. What are some beach souvenirs that tourists can buy?

8. Which seas and oceans have you seen?

9. Which was most stormy? Which was most calm? Most beautiful?

10. Which ocean or sea was coldest? Which was most warm?

11. What sports can be played on the beach or in the water?

12. What kind of bathing suit do you usually wear?
    Do you have a favorite bathing suit?

13. What do you usually bring to the beach?

14. What precautions do you take to avoid being sunburned?

15. Do you like to swim? Do you prefer swimming in a pool or an ocean? Why?

16. What movies have you seen that celebrate the beach or surfing?

17. Have you ever tried to bodysurf? What happened?

18. Have you ever tried to use a boogie board?
    A surfboard? What happened?

VOCABULARY

Read the vocabulary list aloud. Then, with the help of your conversation partner, write five sentences about the beach.

souvenir..

stormy..

calm..

surfboard..

dolphin...

shark..

jellyfish sting...

lotion..

umbrella...

hurricane...

tsunami..

THE CONVERSATION CONTINUES...

1. Have you ever gone snorkeling? Scuba-diving? Did you enjoy it?

2. Have you ever gone swimming in the ocean at night?

3. Have you ever seen dolphins in the water? What were they doing?

4. Have you ever seen sharks in the water? How did you feel?

5. Have you ever been stung by a jellyfish? How did you treat the sting?

6. Have you ever gone saltwater fishing? Did you catch anything?

7. What birds have you seen at the beach? Pelicans? Seagulls? Other?

8. Can you describe a memorable day at the beach? What happened?

9. Why do so many children love going to the beach?

10. What activities have you done with children on a beach?

11. Have you ever built a sand castle? How big was it?

12. Have you ever collected shells? What is your favorite type of shell?

13. Have you ever kept something you found at the beach? What is a beachcomber?

14. On the beach, what is the difference between high tide and low tide?

15. What are some threats to clean beaches? How can we help protect them?

16. Have you ever seen a beach after a hurricane or tsunami? What did you see?

17. Do you prefer going to the beach alone, with your partner, your family, or with a group of friends? Why?

18. What islands or beaches would you like to visit? Why?

REMEMBER...

Explore

Have fun

Be active

Write the meaning of three of the following sayings and proverbs.

He has buried his head in the sand.

She's in deep water.

It's hard to swim against the current.

Sink or swim.

He's riding a wave of popularity at the moment.

The ocean does not choose its trash.—Japanese

1. ....

2. ....

3. ....

QUOTATIONS

Read aloud all the quotations. Pick your favorite and explain to your partner why it is your favorite.

1. "In every curving beach, in every grain of sand, there is the story of the earth."
   —Rachel Carson (1907–1964), biologist and environmentalist

2. "The sea does not reward those who are too anxious, too greedy, or too impatient. One should lie empty, open, choiceless as a beach–waiting for a gift from the sea."
   —Anne Morrow Lindberg (1906–2001), writer

3. "Time and tide wait for no man."
   —Geoffrey Chaucer (1343–1400), English author

4. "On vacations: We hit the sunny beaches where we occupy ourselves keeping the sun off our skin, the saltwater off our bodies, and the sand out of our belongings."
   —Erma Bombeck (1927–1996), America humorist

5. "When one tugs at a single thing in nature, he finds it attached to the rest of the world."
   —John Muir (1838–1914), environmentalist

6. "I hate vacations. If you can build buildings, why sit on a beach?"
   —Phillip Johnson (1906–2005), American architect

7. "A beach not only permits inertia, but enforces it, thus neatly eliminating all problems of guilt. It is now the only place in our overly active world that does."
   —John Kenneth Galbraith (1908–), American diplomat, economist

8. "You can tell all you need to about a society from how it treats animals and beaches."
   —Frank Deford (1938–), sports commentator

9. "The sea never changes and its works, for all the talk of men, are wrapped in mystery."
   —Joseph Conrad (1857–1924), novelist

ON YOUR OWN

Find a picture in a magazine or pamphlet which shows a beach you would like to visit

Bring the picture to class to share with others. Describe the scene to others in your small group.

> "Thanksgiving Day…is the one day that is truly American."
>
> O. Henry (1862–1910),
> American short story writer

24

HOLIDAYS AND CELEBRATIONS

SHARING MEMORIES

Holidays bring people together. Talk with your partner about the holidays of your lives.

1. When you were a child, what was your favorite holiday or festival? Why? What did you enjoy?

2. What inspired this holiday? What usually happens on this holiday?

3. What are some holy days in your religious tradition?

4. When is the New Year observed in your homeland? How is the New Year celebrated? Which calendar do you use?

5. In your native land, is there a special day to honor mothers? Fathers? Children?

6. Is there a special day to honor all ancestors? How is it celebrated?

7. Can you think of any fantasy figure, such as Santa Claus, connected to holiday celebrations? What is the fantasy figure like? What does this fantasy figure do?

8. Do any holidays in your native country celebrate the end of a war? Which war? How do you mark the occasion?

9. Do any holidays honor war veterans? How are they honored?

10. Can you think of some national holidays to honor the birthdays of famous leaders? Who are the leaders? What did they do?

11. What are the official legal holidays in your native country?

12. Can you tell me about other special days, perhaps social holidays or days of personal significance, that most individuals celebrate in your country?

13. Which holidays have special foods which accompany the celebration?

14. What are the 10 official, legal holidays in the United States?

15. What are some popular social holidays, sometimes called "Hallmark holidays," here?

VOCABULARY

Please circle the words that you know. Use them to write three questions.

celebrate ....

honor ....

festival ....

parade ....

fireworks ....

carol ....

accompany ....

celebration ....

costumes ....

veteran ....

ancestor ....

homesick ....

fantasy ....

ritual ....

procession ....

REMEMBER...

Celebrate

Be curious

Be yourself

SAYINGS

Read the common sayings and proverbs below. Can you add two more?

The more the merrier.

When the boss is away, work becomes a holiday.—Portuguese

Time spent laughing is time spent with the gods.—Japanese

Enjoy yourself. It's later than you think.—Chinese

Shared joys are doubled; shared sorrows are halved.

(Add your own) ....

(Add your own) ....

THE CONVERSATION CONTINUES...

1. What are some traditional gifts for Valentine's Day? How do you celebrate it?

2. Do you know what happens in the comic movie *Groundhog Day*?

3. Which holidays include special songs, dances, or costumes?

4. Do you have a favorite song or dance linked to a holiday? Which? Do you own any collection of holiday songs?

5. Which holidays often include fireworks? Parades? Caroling?

6. What are three special holiday activities for children?

7. On what holidays, do people traditionally put on costumes? Did you celebrate a holiday similar to Halloween in your native country?

8. What are some holidays that occur in the Spring?

9. Do you have a favorite Spring holiday? What is the holiday? How is it celebrated?

10. In your native land, is there a winter holiday which uses lots of lights near the winter solstice? What is the holiday? How is it celebrated?

11. Now that you are in the United States, do you still celebrate the same holidays?

12. Can you think of some movies centered around a holiday? Do you have a favorite movie to watch during the holidays? Why?

13. What is your favorite holiday? How do you celebrate it?

14. Did you celebrate July 4 last year? Thanksgiving? What did you do?

15. Have you seen any new holidays created, or dropped, in your lifetime? Which ones?

16. Do you feel more homesick near holiday time? What do you especially miss?

17. Why do you think so many people find the holiday season stressful?

18. What are your best tips to make holidays a positive experience?

19. Would you like to add, or create, a new holiday? What? Why? How would you like to celebrate this new holiday?

QUOTATIONS

Read aloud all the quotations. Pick your favorites and discuss.

1. "A feast is made for laughter."
   —Ecclesiastes 10:19.

2. "You can't have Thanksgiving without turkey. That's like Fourth of July without apple pie, or Friday without two pizzas."
   —Joey (Matt LeBlanc) on *Friends*, an American situation comedy (sitcom) series

3. "Happy, happy Christmas, that win us back to the delusions of our childhood days, recall to the old man the pleasures of his youth, and transport the traveler back to his own fireside and quiet home."
   —Charles Dickens (1812–1870) English novelist

4. "I was an atheist for a while, but I gave it up. No holidays!"
   —Henry Youngman (1906–1998) American comedian

5. "In the old days, it was not called the Holiday Season; the Christians called it 'Christmas' and went to church; the Jews called it 'Hanukkah' and went to synagogue; the atheists went to parties and drank."
   —Dave Barry (1947–) American comedian

6. "Christmas is the season when gifts are gladly given, happily received, and cheerfully refunded."
   —Evan Esar (1899–1995), American humorist

7. "April 1: This is the day upon which we are reminded of what we are on the other three hundred and sixty-four."
   —Mark Twain (1835–1910) humorist

8. "Live your life while you have it. Life is a splendid gift—there's nothing small about it."
  —Florence Nightingale (1820–1910), Founder of the Red Cross

9. "Yes, Virginia, there is a Santa Claus. He exists as certainly as love and generosity and devotion exist."
  —Francis B. Church (1839–1906), publisher and editor

10. "Today is Valentine's Day, or, as men like to call it, Extortion Day!"
  —Jay Leno (1950–), late night American television comedian

11. "To many people holidays are not voyages of discovery, but a ritual of reassurance."
  —Phillip Andrew Adams (1939–), Australian broadcaster

MONTH ....

M	Tu	W	Th	F	Sa	Su

ON YOUR OWN

Using the grid at right, create a calendar for the month of your birth, showing your birthday and other holidays.

On separate sheets of paper, create a 12-month calendar showing the days you celebrate and official American holidays.

"In the 21st century, you will:

- **Do more**
- **Know more**
- **Have more**
- **Travel more**
- **See more**
- **Be more**

Than people in any previous generation in any human civilization."

ALLAN NEUHARTH
(1924–), publisher of USA Today

Modern Times

25

WHAT DO YOU THINK?

AGREEING TO DISAGREE

Life would be boring if we all agreed all the time. The following phrases let you state your position clearly while keeping the conversation friendly. Read all phrases aloud.

Expressing agreement	…or disagreement
I agree.	I don't agree.
That's right.	Sorry, I disagree.
Absolutely.	I can't go along with that.
That's true.	That's not completely true.
I believe that.	I don't believe that.
That's a good idea.	That's wrong. What about x, y, or z ?
That's right on target.	That's way off base. That's quite a stretch.
I concur.	I can't agree. On the contrary/ I dissent.
That's valid.	That's invalid. That's not always true.
I accept that.	I reject that. I can't accept that. I partly agree.
I support that.	I can't support that. I reject that idea.
That idea has my vote.	I have a different idea./I have a better idea.
I definitely agree.	I beg to differ. I see things differently.
I strongly agree.	That doesn't make sense. Is that logical?
I couldn't agree more.	That seems simplistic. I think you are wrong here.
You go, girl!	I can't go there!

VOCABULARY

Circle the words that you already know. Look up the other words.

agree ....

disagree ....

concur ....

assume...

solution...

valid..

invalid ....

support ....

assumption ....

response ....

accept..

reject ....

deny ....

results ....

consequences ....

AGREE? OR DISAGREE? PART I

Do you agree or disagree with the following proverbs? Why? Discuss with your partner.

1. The best things in life are free.

2. Children should be seen and not heard.

3. Spare the rod and spoil the child.

4. Money is the root of all evil.

5. Honesty is the best policy.

6. It's better to have loved and lost than never to have loved at all.

7. Behind every successful man there's a woman.

8. The end justifies the means.

9. Winning is everything.

10. Better to be a live dog than a dead lion.

11. Persistence pays.

12. There is no good war and no bad peace.

13. Your best friend is yourself.

14. Never judge a movie by its preview.

15. You can't keep a good man down.

16. A closed mouth catches no flies.

17. The best defense is a good offense.

18. Money makes the world go round.

ACTIVITY

Choose a topic about which you and your conversation partner disagree. Spend five minutes discussing your opinions in a friendly, respectful way. Use some of the phrases at the beginning of this chapter to keep the conversation flowing.

SEEKING CLARIFICATION

Sometimes we need more information. Read each of these phrases aloud to your partner.

So? What do you mean?

Can you rephrase that? Why do you say that?

Can you give another example? Have you considered…?

What if the situation were a bit different? What if…?

Do you think that is the only reason/cause/explanation? How far would you go?

Are you sure? Why are you so sure?

What's your source for that bit of information? How do you know?

Can you imagine some alternatives? Is there another possibility?

AGREE? OR DISAGREE? PART II

Consider each of the following common statements, attitudes, or proverbs. Which statement of agreement or disagreement best expresses your reaction?

1. Seeing is believing.
2. Appearances are deceiving.
3. Beauty promises happiness.
4. Be good and you will be happy.
5. No pain, no gain.
6. No pain, no pain.
7. The bigger, the better.
8. Less is more.
9. Cream rises to the top.
10. The unexpected always happens.
11. You get what you pay for.
12. A penny saved is a penny earned.
13. Two can live as cheaply as one.
14. Bad news travels fast.
15. Liars should have good memories.
16. Life is not a popularity contest.
17. Counting your money is how you keep score.
18. You can't take it with you.
19. Time heals all wounds.

20. Never forget; never forgive.

21. Don't throw your pearls before swine.

22. A donkey prefers hay to gold.

QUOTATIONS

Here are some strong statements from a variety of prominent individuals. What do you think? Do you completely agree? Mostly disagree? Feel neutral? Strongly disagree? Is the statement an exaggeration? How? Please give examples and reasons to support your point of view as you discuss these statements with your partner.

1. "True love is like ghosts, which everybody talks about and few have seen."
   —Francois Duc De La Rochefoucauld (1613–1680), French writer

2. "A man will fight harder for his interest than for his rights."
   —Napoleon (1769–1821), French leader and military genius

3. "Today's audience knows more about what's on television than what's in life."
   —Larry Gilbert (1928–) actor, writer, and producer

4. "Art is the proper task of life."
   —Friedrich Nietzsche (1844–1900) German philosopher

5. "Nobody minds having what is too good for them."
   —Jane Austen (1775–1821), English novelist

6. "Nothing is so dangerous as an ignorant friend; a wise enemy is much better."
   —Jean de La Fontaine (1621–1695), French poet

7. "Permissiveness is the principle of treating children as if they were adults; and the tactic of making sure they will never reach that stage."
   —Dr. Thomas Szasz (1921–) psychiatrist

8. "Nationalism: An infantile disease. It is the measles of mankind."
   —Albert Einstein (1879–1955), *Time* Magazine's Man of the 20th Century

9. "Christmas is the time when kids tell Santa what they want and adults pay for it. Deficits are when adults tell government what they want and their kids pay for it."
   —Richard Lamm (1935–), former Governor of Colorado

10. "If two ride on a horse, one must ride behind."
    —William Shakespeare (1564–1616), great English playwright

11. "Experience is the name everyone gives their mistakes."
    —Oscar Wilde (1854–1900), Irish playwright

12. "We make war so we may live in peace."
    —Aristotle (384–322 B.C.E.), Greek philosopher

"I never learned from a man who agreed with me."

Robert Heinlein (1907–1988), American writer

ON YOUR OWN

Scan the editorial page of a publication. Pick a letter to the editor, editorial, or op-ed that "sounds right" to you. Bring it to class and explain your choice.

OR

What are some controversial issues in your country? Make a list of five topics that people are debating. Which one do you think is most important? Why?

26
CHANGE

SHARING NOTES

All of us have to deal with change. Sometimes it's fun; sometimes it's hard. Share some of your experiences with your class partner.

1. How has your neighborhood changed in the last five years?

2. How have clothing fashions changed during your lifetime?

3. Do you dress differently than you did five years ago? How?

4. How have your looks changed in the last ten years?

5. What's your reaction to a woman changing her looks with make-up? Hair dye? Plastic surgery?

6. What about men? Is it okay if men use make-up? Hair dye? Plastic surgery?

7. If you could have a free makeover, what physical changes would you seek? Why?

8. Can you name three changes important technological changes in your life?

9. What type of technology has helped the most people? Why?

10. Do you try and keep up with technological changes? What skills have you added in the last five years?

11. What social changes have happened in your native country in your lifetime?

12. What political changes have happened in your native country in your lifetime?

13. What is a custom or tradition that you would like to change in your native country? Why?

14. What social changes you would like to see in America?

15. What three political changes would you like to happen in the world?

16. Has nature changed in the last 100 years? How?

17. Has human nature changed in the last 100 years? If so, how?

VOCABULARY

Circle three words. Does your class partner know their meanings?

fashion..

makeover...

inevitable...

adjust..

resist ....

resistance...

rehabilitation...

optimistic..

pessimistic ....

resilient..

PROVERBS

Have you heard any of these? Circle the ones with which you agree.

Don't change horses in midstream.

A leopard can't change its spots.

Change is in the air.

It's time for a change.

A bird in the hand is worth two in the bush.

The grass is always greener on the other side of the fence.

Old habits die hard.

Change for change's sake.

You can't make an omelette without breaking eggs.

Out with the old and in with the new.

You can't teach an old dog new tricks.

It's a woman's prerogative to change her mind.

THE CONVERSATION CONTINUES...

1. Can you name anything which is the same as it was 100 years ago? What?

2. What personal changes would you welcome?

3. Are there personal changes that you fear? What?

4. If you could stop time and keep everything the same, would you? Why?

5. What change in your life did you easily adjust to?

6. What change did you resist? Did it work? Was resistance helpful?

7. Have any of your basic ideas changed in the last five years? What?

8. Do you believe that rehabilitation is possible for violent criminals?

9. What changes do you think will happen in the next five years? Why?

10. What changes do you hope for in the next decade? 100 years?

REMEMBER...

Be encouraging

Be honest

Be kind

11. Have your ideas about family changed as you have grown older? How?

12. Have your ideas about God changed as you have grown older? How?

13. Have your ideas about happiness changed as you have grown older? How?

14. Are you more optimistic or more pessimistic than you used to be? Why? Can you give an example?

15. Can you share some tips for becoming more resilient amidst change?

QUOTATIONS

Which quotation is your favorite? Do you disagree with any quotation?

1. "The universe is change."
   —Marcus Aurelius (121–180), Roman Emperor

2. "Never doubt that a small group of thoughtful, committed citizens can change the world. Indeed it is the only thing that ever has."
   —Margaret Mead (1907–1978), anthropologist

3. "Change your thoughts and you change the world."
   —Norman Vincent Peale (1898–1993), clergyman

4. "There is nothing like returning to a place that remains unchanged to find the ways in which you yourself have altered."
   —Nelson Mandela (1918–), African Leader

5. "Things do not change; we change."
   —Henry David Thoreau (1817–1862), essayist

6. "Time may change me, but I can't change time."
   —David Bowie (1947–), English musician/actor

7. "We did not change as we grew older; we just became more clearly ourselves."
   —Lynn Hall (1937–), prolific author of children's books

ON YOUR OWN

Before next class, choose a place which is special to you and write a few sentences about how it has changed since you were a child.

....

....

....

....

8. "A foolish consistency is the hobgoblin of little minds."
   —Ralph Waldo Emerson (1803–1882), writer

9. "To modernize is to adopt and to adapt, but it is also to re-create."
   —Octavio Paz (1914–1998), Mexican writer and diplomat

10. "It is not the strongest of the species that survive, nor the most intelligent, but the one most responsive to change."
    —Charles Darwin (1809–1882), naturalist

11. "Make change your friend."
    —Bill Clinton (1946–), 42nd U.S. President

12. "A man needs a little madness, or else he never dares cut the rope and be free."
    —Nikos Kazantzakis (1883–1957), Greek writer, Nobel Prize winner

13. "We must be the change we want to see in the world."
    —Gandhi (1869–1948), Indian statesman

27
CLOTHES AND FASHION

SHARING VIEWS

Styles and fashions change, but the desire to surround ourselves with
beauty remains. Discuss clothing options with your conversation partner.

1. What are you wearing today? Where did you get your favorite piece
   of clothing?
2. Do you usually dress casually or formally?
3. Do you prefer conservative, shabby, or trendy clothes? Why?
4. Do you find dressing for work a chore, a choice, or a pleasure? Why?
5. When picking clothes, are you drawn to certain colors? Which?
6. How often do you shop for clothes? Do you have a favorite day or
   time?
7. Do you like to window shop for clothes? Where do you go?
8. Can you suggest stores that sell quality clothes at reasonable prices?
9. Are clothing styles, or stores, different in your native country than
   here? How?
10. Do you have a favorite outfit? Where do you go in it?
11. How do you accessorize? Do you have a favorite accessory?
12. Is there a traditional dress in your native country? Can you
    describe it?
13. How often do you get dressed up? For what occasions?
14. Do you dress differently in the U.S. than you did in your native
    country?
15. Do people in your native country tend to dress more conservatively
    or more showy?
16. Have you ever worn a uniform for work or school? Can you
    describe it?
17. What is an example of something you would never wear? Why?
18. Whom do you think of as being fashionable or chic? Why?

VOCABULARY

Please circle the words that you know. Use them to write three questions.

fashion...

chic...

elegant...

shabby...

trend...

trendy..

despot...

icon ....

designer...

accessory...

NOTES & QUESTIONS

....

....

....

....

....

....

....

....

PROVERBS

Read the common sayings and proverbs below. Can you add two more?

Clothes make the man.—Talmud

Clothes hide the blemish.—Yiddish

Dress up a monkey like a bishop, it's still a monkey.—Japanese

Style is substance.—American

When it's torn, it can't be worn.—Persian

As for clothes, the newer the better;
as for friends, the older the better.—Korean

You get what you pay for.—Greek

THE CONVERSATION CONTINUES...

1. Which materials do you prefer to wear?

2. Are you allergic to any materials?

3. Do you sew? Have you patched jeans or other clothes?

4. What do you do with old clothes? Do you give them away? Sell them at a garage sale?

5. Can you describe some clothes that would clash? What is a fashion faux pas?

6. What type of clothes, jewelry, or furniture do you find tacky? Shabby? Ugly?

7. If you were the "fashion police," what would you get rid of? Why?

8. Who are some fashion icons? Can you think of some "fashion forward" people?

9. Do you have a favorite fashion designer? Why?

10. What is the difference between style and fashion?

11. Have you ever felt that fashion was a despot or tyrant? How?

12. Who taught you how to dress? Who was your role model? Why?

13. Do you dress differently from your parents? How?

14. Do your children dress differently from you? How?

15. What do you usually notice about clothes? What catches your eye?

16. Is there anything you don't allow your children to wear? What? Why?

17. Who do you consider the best-dressed celebrity? The worst? Why?

18. Should people be allowed to wear whatever they want whenever they want? Why or why not?

19. Can you share your five best fashion tips with me?

QUOTATIONS

Circle the quotations you like, and connect the expression to your life.

1. "Be not the first by whom the new are tried
   Nor yet the last to lay the old aside."
   —Alexander Pope (1688–1744), English poet

2. "The fashion wears out more apparel than the man."
   —William Shakespeare (1564–1616), English playwright, poet

3. "Now I can wear high heels again."
   —Nicole Kidman, (1967–) actress, after her divorce.

4. "I dress for women, and undress for men."
   —Angie Dickinson (1931–) actress

5. "I only put clothes on so that I'm not naked when I go out shopping."
   —Julia Roberts (1967–) actress and movie star

6. "Naked people have little or no influence in society."
   —Mark Twain (1835–1910)

7. "He is ill clothed that is bare of virtue."
   —Benjamin Franklin (1706–1790) statesman

8. "In your community, your reputation matters. In a strange place, your clothing counts."
   —Talmud

9. "We are all Adam's children, but silk makes the difference."
   —Thomas Fuller (1608–1661), English historian and religious leader

10. "Beware of all enterprises that require new clothes."
    —Henry David Thoreau (1817–1860) American philosopher

11. "The man who inspects the saddle blanket instead of the horse is stupid; most stupid is the man who judges another man by his clothes or circumstances."
    —Seneca the Younger (4 B.C.E.–65 A.D.), Roman statesmen and writer

12. "If most of us are ashamed of shabby clothes and shoddy furniture, let us be more ashamed of shabby ideas and shoddy philosophies."
    —Albert Einstein (1879–1955), scientist and philosopher

13. "A thing of beauty is a joy–until the fashion changes."
    —Evan Esar (1899–1995), writer

14. "I base most of my fashion taste on what doesn't itch."
    —Gilda Radner (1946–1989), television comedian

15. "Fashion: That, not necessarily beautiful, which makes what preceded it look stodgy, foolish, or inexpensive."
    —Leo Rosten (1908–1997), author

16. "You may judge a flower or a butterfly by its looks, but not a human being…Only fools judge men by their outside."
    —Radindranath Tagore (1861–1941), Indian poet, Nobel Prize winner

ON YOUR OWN

Pick a favorite outfit or piece of clothing. At right, write about the outfit: where it was made, how you got it, and why you like it. Share your short essay with classmates.

28

APPRECIATING PHYSICAL BEAUTY

SHARING VIEWS

Most people hope they are attractive to others. What is beautiful to you? Share your thoughts with your class partner. Feel free to skip questions or add questions. Have fun!

1. Who are some women that you find beautiful?

2. Whom do you consider elegant? Whom do you consider stylish?

3. Which woman is the closest to your ideal?

4. What three characteristics about her do you find most attractive?

5. Who are some men that you find handsome? Which is the closest to your ideal?

6. What three characteristics about him do you find most attractive?

7. Who are, or were, some "sex symbols" in your country? Why?

8. Can you name ugly celebrities or people? What makes them ugly?

9. Where can you go to watch people and "feast your eyes"?

10. Do you use cosmetics? If so, when did you start? Who taught you to use lipstick, mascara, etc?

11. Where do you shop when you want to buy something to make you look better? Why do you shop there?

12. What kinds of cosmetics are common for young women in your country?

13. Do you think women are more attractive when they wear makeup? How?

14. Do you read fashion or style magazines? Which ones? How have clothing fashions changed recently?

15. On a scale of 1-10, how important is physical attractiveness to you in a lover?

15. Do you believe in love at first sight? Why?

Circle three words you know. Use each of the three in sentences which you tell your partner.

balance...

athletic...

pierced...

muscular...

enhance..

cosmetics..

beard..

irresistible...

trim..

plastic surgery...

mustache..

....

....

....

....

....

....

....

PROVERBS

Read aloud each of the following proverbs. Then, choose one and explain it to your class partner.

Beauty attracts. Personality keeps.

Love is blind.—English

Even pockmarks may look like dimples.—Japanese

The eyes are the window of the soul.—English

In love, beauty counts for more than good advice.—Latin

Beauty is as Beauty does.—American

Inside every fat person is a thin person trying to get out.—American

THE CONVERSATION CONTINUES...

1. Do you notice women's hairstyles? What does long hair say? Short hair? What styles do you prefer?

2. Do you pay attention to men's hair? What does baldness convey to you? Long hair? What styles do you prefer?

3. Do you usually think beards look good? What about mustaches? Long sideburns?

4. Is it common in your homeland for women to have pierced ears? At what age?

5. Do you find permanent piercings or markings attractive? Do they enhance attractiveness?

6. How have notions of beauty changed in your native country in the last 50 years?

7. How are notions of beauty and fashion different from the U.S.?

8. How widespread is plastic surgery in your homeland? Is Botox popular? Why?

9. Do you know anyone who has ever been to a plastic surgeon? What operation was performed? Was the person more attractive to you?

10. In literature, who are some of the women of great physical beauty who were considered irresistible by men? Can you describe one from your native country?

11. Who are some men, in literature or myth, of great physical attractiveness whom women found irresistible? Can you describe one?

12. What physical features do you appreciate, and find attractive, in a women?

13. What makes a man attractive to you? What physical features do you appreciate?

14. What do you find beautiful in nature? What animals do you find beautiful?

15. What makes an object beautiful? Is it balance? Is it harmony? Is it color?

16. What makes someone beautiful? What is beauty?

QUOTATIONS

With the help of your partner, decide what is meant by #7 and #12. Do you agree with these ideas?

1. "Beauty's but skin deep."
   —John Davies (1565–1618), English Dramatist

2. "If eyes were made for seeing, Then Beauty is its own excuse for being."
   —Ralph Waldo Emerson (1803–1882), American essayist

3. "Beauty is truth, truth beauty,—that is all ye know on earth, and all ye need to know."
   —John Keats (1795–1821), English poet

4. "Why should beauty be suspect?"
   —Auguste Renoir (1841–1919), French artist

5. "If the nose of Cleopatra had been shorter, the whole face of the earth would have been changed."
   —Blaise Pascal (1623–1662), French philosopher

6. "There is no excellent beauty that hath not some strangeness in proportion."
   —Francis Bacon (1561–1626), English philosopher

7. "To men a man is but a mind. Who cares what face he carries or what form he wears? But woman's body is the woman."
   —Ambrose Bierce (1842–1914), American writer

8. "There's so much to say, but your eyes keep interrupting me."
   —Christopher Morley (1890–1957), American writer

9. "Beauty and folly are generally companions."
   —Baltasar Gracian (1601–1658) Spanish philosopher

10. "I'm a very physical person. People don't credit me with much of a brain, so why should I disillusion them?"
    —Sylvester Stallone (1946–), film star and director

11. "I require only three things of a man. He must be handsome, ruthless, and stupid."
    —Dorothy Parker (1893–1967), American writer

12. "Beautiful bodies and beautiful personalities rarely go together."
    —Carl Gustav Jung (1875–1961), psychologist

13. "Just standing around looking beautiful is so boring, really boring, so boring."
    —Michelle Pfeiffer (1957–), actress

ON YOUR OWN

Cut out and bring to class a picture from a magazine of a female or male whom you find attractive.

Write four sentences which express your opinions on what makes that person beautiful or handsome.

....

....

....

....

"When a woman is talking to you, listen to what she says with her eyes."

Victor Hugo (1802–1885), French novelist

29

DATING

SHARING VIEWS

Everyone has questions about dating. Share some of your dating advice with your class partner.

1. How old were you when you went on your first date?

2. Where did you go? Were you alone or was there a chaperone?

3. Were any gifts exchanged? Flowers?

4. How is dating different in your country than in the U.S.?

5. When do people start dating? Is it different for males and females? Why?

6. Are there any courtship traditions in your country?

7. What are some advantages of your country's courtship tradition?

8. What are some advantages of the dating style in the United States?

9. Who should pay for the date? Should the date be "a Dutch treat"?

10. What should you wear on a date? How do you prepare for a date?

11. Are you currently seeing anyone?

12. Do you date? How often do you date?

13. What places do you recommend for a romantic date in our city?

14. What do you like to do on a date? Dinner? Movie? Dancing?

15. Are there any "rules" to dating? What are they?

16. What questions are you likely to ask on a first date?

17. What is the best date you have ever been on?

18. What is the worst date you have ever been on? Did you have "mad money?"

19. What are some good date movies? Why?

20. Have you ever been on a blind date? Who set you up? Did you enjoy yourself?

21. Do you think blind dates are a good idea?

22. Where have your friends met their lovers?

VOCABULARY

Circle the words that you know. Write definitions for at least five words.

courtship ....

fate ....

chaperone ....

double date ....

blind ....

blind date ....

Dutch treat...

rain check...

walk out..

personal ad ....

stood up ....

matchmaker ....

PROVERBS

Circle the ones you think are true.

A kiss tells more than a whole book.—Ukrainian

If you want to be loved, be lovable.—Roman

Beauty is but one layer.—Japanese

Those that can't love, flatter.

If you have money, you are wise
and good-looking and can sing well too.—Yiddish

You have to kiss a lot of frogs before you find a prince.

REMEMBER...

Be yourself

Have fun

Make good mistakes

THE CONVERSATION CONTINUES...

1. What qualities do you look for in a person on a date?

2. How can you tell if a couple is compatible?

3. How would you ask for a rain check?

4. Why do people enjoy looking at personal ads in a newspaper?

5. Have you ever been on computer dating sites? What did you notice? Have you met anyone?

6. If you could go on a date with anyone in the world, who would it be?

7. Have you ever gone on a double date? Was it fun?

8. Have you ever walked out on a date? Why? Have you ever stood anyone up?

9. What is your idea of a great date?

10. Have you ever played matchmaker for a friend? Were you successful?

11. Would you rather be the flame or the moth? Why?

12. Do you believe a date can change your fate?

13. Do you have any dating tips you would like to share?

QUOTATIONS

Do any of these make you smile? Which ones? Circle your favorite.

1. "A man's kiss is his signature."
   —Mae West (1893–1980), American actress/movie star

2. "The perjured oaths of lovers carry no penalty."
   —Syrus (85–43 B.C.E.), Roman philosopher

3. "Anyone who says he can see through women is missing a lot."
   —Groucho Marx (1895–1977), movie star

4. "A woman has got to love a bad man once or twice in her life, to be thankful for a good one."
   —Marjorie Kinnan Rawlings (1896–1953), novelist

5. "I was born when you kissed me. I died when you left me. I lived a few weeks while you loved me."
   —Humphrey Bogart to Ingrid Bergman in *Casablanca*

6. "Sex without love is merely healthy exercise."
   —Robert A. Heinlein (1907–1988), science fiction writer

7. "I've only slept with the men I've been married to. How many women can make that claim?"
   —Elizabeth Taylor (1932–), movie star married eight times

8. "My success has allowed me to strike out with a higher class of women."
   —Woody Allen (1935–), American comedian, actor, and director

9. "You're not too smart, are you? I like that in a man."
   —Kathleen Turner, actress, to William Hurt, actor, in *Body Heat*

10. "Listen, I appreciate this whole seduction thing you've got going, but let me give you a tip. I'm a sure thing."
    —Julia Roberts to Richard Gere in *Pretty Woman* (1990)

11. "To fall in love is to create a religion that has a fallible god."
    —Jorge Luis Borges (1899–1986), Nobel Prize winner, writer

12. "Take away love, and our earth is a tomb."
    —Robert Browning (1812–1889), English romantic poet

13. "Love is so short and forgetting is so long."
    —Pablo Neruda (1904–1973), Chilean poet

14. "Love is not just looking at each other; it's looking in the same direction."
    —Antoine de Saint-Exupery (1900–1944), French writer

ON YOUR OWN

Write a personal ad for yourself or a friend.

....

....

....

....

....

....

....

....

30

ENJOYING MONEY

SHARING EXPERIENCES

We all deal with money. What experiences have you had? Share your knowledge about money with your class partner.

1. What is the name of money in your native country?
   What does it look like?

2. How much is a dollar in your native country's currency?

3. How much does seeing a movie cost? A gallon of gas? Lunch?

4. Can you compare shopping in the United States with your native country?

5. What are some bargains in your native country? Why?

6. Are you a thrifty shopper? Can you give an example?

7. Do you know someone who collects loose change? What do you do with the coins?

8. Do you know anybody who collects coins as a hobby?

9. Do you have any shopping tips for bargain hunting?

10. Are you an impulsive shopper or do you shop with a list?

11. When do you like to splurge? On what?

12. Do you prefer to go shopping by yourself or with someone else? Why?

13. Do you have a favorite mall, shopping center, or market?

14. Have you ever wasted money? How?

15. How often do you go out to restaurants?
    What do you look for in restaurants?

16. Are you a tipper? What percentage do you usually leave for good service?

17. Can you think of some extravagant ways to spend money?

18. Have you ever felt "buyer's remorse"? When? What did you do?

VOCABULARY

Circle five words you know. Use each in a sentence for your partner.

currency ....

coin ....

thrifty ....

frugal..

impulsive ....

extravagant ....

remorse ....

buyer's remorse...

tip ....

tipper...

budget ....

credit ....

pile up ....

debt ....

PROVERBS

Do you agree with all these proverbs? Circle your favorite.

Time is money.—Greek

No one spits on money.—Korean

Without money; without hands.—Ukrainian

Money can bribe the gods.—Chinese

When money talks, truth keeps silent.—Russian

THE CONVERSATION CONTINUES...

1. How do you like to spend money? What are you glad to buy?

2. Do you have a favorite store? Why?

3. Have you ever bought several identical items? Why?

4. Do you have a budget for yourself? Does your family have a budget?

5. How do you keep track of what you spend?
   Do you keep a money diary?

6. Do you have a favorite paper currency or bill? Why do you like it?

7. Do you have a favorite coin? Why do you like it?

8. Do you usually pay bills by check, by credit card, or by computer?

9. Do you usually pay by cash, check, or credit card at stores?

10. If you got a sudden gift of $10,000, what would you buy? Why?

11. When did open your first bank account?
    When did you get your first credit card?

12. Do young people tend to live within their means or above their means? Why?

NOTES & QUESTIONS

....

....

....

....

....

....

....

13. Have your spending habits changed since moving to the United States? How?

14. What are some common reasons that people go into debt?

15. Can you think of five good uses of credit?

16. What are five bad reasons to pile up debt? Why?

17. Do you and your relatives have similar spending habits?

18. What would you buy if you won the lottery for $50 million? Why?

19. What is your personal spending philosophy?

QUOTATIONS

Read aloud all the quotations. Explain your favorite to your partner.

1. "When it's a question of money, everybody is of the same religion."—Voltaire (1694–1778)

2.. "He that is of the opinion that money will do everything may well be suspected of doing everything for money."—Benjamin Franklin (1706–1790), American statesmen and face on the U.S. $100 bill

3. "Money often costs too much."
—Ralph Waldo Emerson (1803–1882), American philosopher

4. "The golden age only comes to men when they have forgotten gold."—G.K. Chesterton (1874–1936), English writer

5. "When I was young I thought that money was the most important thing in life; now that I'm old I know that it is."
—Oscar Wilde (1854–1900), Anglo-Irish playwright

6. "Money: A blessing that is of no advantage to us excepting when we part with it."
—Ambrose Bierce (1842–1914), American writer

7. "The lack of money is the root of all evil."
—George Bernard Shaw (1856–1950), Irish writer

8. "Why is there so much month left at the end of the money?"
—John Barrymore (1882–1942), acting legend

9. "Money cannot buy health, but I'd settle for a diamond-studded wheel chair."—Dorothy Parker (1893–1967), American writer

10. "I don't like money, actually, but it quiets my nerves."
—Joe Louis (1914–1981), world heavyweight champion

11. "I'm living so far beyond my income that we may almost be said to be living apart."—William Cowper (1721–1800), English poet

12. "It's a kind of spiritual snobbery that makes people believe they can be happy without money."
—Albert Camus (1913–1960), French novelist and Nobel winner

13. "I'd like to live like a poor man with lots of money."
—Pablo Picasso (1881–1993), Spanish painter

14. "I have enough money to last me the rest of my life, unless I buy something."
—Jackie Mason (1931–) American stand-up comedian

ON YOUR OWN

Write four sentences which reflect your attitudes about money.

1. ....

....

2. ....

....

3. ....

....

4. ....

....

31

EATING OUT

SHARING EXPERIENCES

Do you know some good restaurants? Share with others in your class what you have learned about eating out.

1. Do you look forward to eating out? Why?

2. Where are some places to eat out in your neighborhood?

3. What kinds of ethnic food do you enjoy? Do you have a favorite dish?

4. Do you prefer eating out with a single person or with a group?

5. Do you remember eating out as a child? Where did you go?

6. Do you think eating out is only for special occasions?

7. Do you drink alcohol when you eat out? Do you have a favorite drink?

8. What kind of appetizers do you like? Do you have a favorite appetizer?

9. Do you regularly eat out with friends? How often do eat out?

10. Do you eat fast food? What do you usually order?

11. Why do you think fast food restaurants are so popular?

12. Do you have a favorite fast food restaurant? Why?

13. What are some downsides to eating at fast food restaurants?

14. What is your favorite cuisine? What dishes do you adore?

15. What do you look for on a menu? What are some signs of a good restaurant?

16. What price range do you usually look for in a restaurant?

17. Do you have a favorite fine dining restaurant?
    What makes the restaurant special?

18. What are restaurants like in your country?
    Can you describe the atmosphere?

19. In your opinion, what qualities make a good waiter? A good valet?

VOCABULARY

Are any of these words new to you? Circle them. Does your partner know their meaning? Can you figure out their meaning?

menu ....

fast food chains ....

reservation ....

busboy ....

waiters ....

tip ....

chef ....

host ....

valet ....

split plate ....

manners ....

THE CONVERSATION CONTINUES...

1. Have you ever ordered off the menu? Why?

2. What can go wrong in a restaurant? Have you ever been disappointed? Have you ever sent food back? Have you ever gotten sick from restaurant food?

3. Do you usually tip waiters? How much?

4. Have you ever worked as a host, chef, waiter, or manager in a restaurant?

5. What was the best part of working in the restaurant? The worst?

6. Do you have a favorite restaurant which serves food from your native country?

7. What language do you use when you order food at that restaurant? Why?

8. How are manners different when dining out in your native country?

9. Did you go out to eat more in your native country than here or vice versa?

10. What are some advantages of home cooking? Do you find cooking a chore or a pleasure?

11. What are some advantages of eating out?

12. How do you judge, evaluate, or rate restaurants?

13. Can you suggest some local restaurants for a romantic dinner?

14. Can you recall any memorable restaurant scenes in famous movies?

15. What are some of your favorite restaurant memories?

QUOTATIONS

Read all the quotations. Circle those with which you agree.

1. "There's no sauce in the world like hunger."
   —Miquel De Cervantes (1547–1616) Spanish writer

2. "Get to know the Chef and you will start to enjoy dining out even more."
   —John Walters, (1938–2001), British radio producer and musician

3. "I judge a restaurant by the bread and the coffee."
   —Burt Lancaster (1915–1994), American actor

4. "I do adore food. If I have any vice it's eating. If I was told I could only eat one food for the rest of my life, I could put up with sausage and mash forever."
   —Colin Baker (1943–), British actor

5. "He may live without books—what is knowledge but grieving?
   He may live without hope—what is hope but deceiving?
   He may live without love—what is passion but pining?
   But where is the man who can live without dining?"
   —Edward Bulwer-Lytton (1831–1891), poet

6. "I have never developed indigestion from eating my words."
   —Winston Churchill (1874–1965), British Prime Minister

7. "I have dined with kings, I've been offered wings. And I've never been too impressed."
   —Bob Dylan (1941–), American folksinger

8. "Gastronomical perfection can be reached in these combinations: one person dining alone, usually upon a couch or a hill side; two people, of no matter what sex or age, dining in a good restaurant; six pcoplc...dining in a good home."
   —M.F.K. Fisher (1908–1992), culinary writer

9. "I've known what it is to be hungry, but I always went right to a restaurant."
   —Ring Lardner (1885–1933) American writer

10. "The best fame is a writer's fame. It's enough to get a table at a good restaurant, but not enough to get you interrupted when you eat."
    —Fran Lebowitz (1950–), writer

11. "The other night I ate at a real nice family restaurant. Every table had an argument going."
    —George Carlin (1937–) American comedian

12. "I learned more from the one restaurant that didn't work than from all the others that were successes."
    —Wolfgang Puck (1949–), chef

13. "Dining is and always was a great artistic opportunity."
    —Frank Lloyd Wright (1867–1959), American architect

14. "One cannot think well, love well, sleep well, if one has not dined well."
    —Virginia Woolf, (1882–1941), English novelist

ON YOUR OWN

With your partner, role play a good waiter and a difficult customer.

Then, role play a pleasant customer and a difficult waiter.

32

GAMBLING AND SPENDING MONEY

TAKING CHANCES

Gambling, or gaming as the popular American industry prefers to call games of chance for money, evokes strong emotions. Take some chances in your interview.

1. Where, if anywhere, do you gamble? For chips? For money?

2. Is gambling legal in your native country?

3. What is the most popular gambling game in your country?

4. Are there any gambling restrictions? What are they? Why?

5. Are there lotteries? Who runs the lotteries?

6. What are some of the pleasures of gambling? Perils?

7. Have you been to Las Vegas? Atlantic City?

8. What were some of your impressions of Las Vegas?

9. Did you gamble in Las Vegas? Which casinos did you like? Why?

10. What is your favorite gambling game? Do you like to play poker? Blackjack? Slots?

11. How would you describe your feeling while gambling?

12. Did your money winnings ever pile up?

13. If you won a big jackpot, say $50,000, what would you buy?

14. Do you have a favorite gambling partner? Why?

15. Do you prefer to gamble during the day or night? Why?

16. Did you win, lose, or break even in Las Vegas? How much?

17. Do you ever gamble on sports? Which? Do you usually win, lose, or break even?

18. Do you think gambling has increased or decreased in the last 10 years?

19. Do you think gambling will increase in the next year? Why?

VOCABULARY

Read each word aloud. Put a check mark next to the words that have a positive meaning, and circle the words that have a negative meaning for you.

thrifty ....

frugal ....

impulsive ....

splurge ....

bet ....

jackpot ....

casino ....

risk ....

compulsive ....

addict ....

remorse ....

debt ....

SAYINGS

Can you think of some other proverbs that apply to gambling?

Gambling is the son of avarice and the father of despair.—French

Don't throw good money after bad.—English

Where there is money, there is danger.—Japanese

There is no better gambling than not to gamble.—German

Put your money where your mouth is.—American

The best throw with the dice
is to throw them away.—t-shirt sold in Las Vegas

The unexpected always happens.—Latin

THE CONVERSATION CONTINUES...

1. What are some common reasons that people go into debt?

2. Can you think of three good uses of credit?

3. What are five bad reasons to pile up debt?

4. Do you think gambling should be legal? Why?

5. What do you think is the secret of gambling's appeal across the centuries?

6. Do you think gambling can be an addiction? How?

7. Have you ever known anyone with a gambling problem? What happened?

8. What are some signs that someone might have a gambling problem?

9. What are some signs of a successful gambler?

10. What are some safe bets in cards? What are some long shots in cards?

REMEMBER...

Be active

Be careful

Have fun

11. What are some risks that you've taken in your life?

12. Do you consider moving to America a smart bet?

13. Do you think life is a gamble? How?

QUOTATIONS

Pick two quotations, memorize them, and use them outside of class.

1. "Every gain must have a loss."
—Francis Bacon (1561–1626), English philosopher

2. "The gambling known as business looks with austere disfavor upon the business known as gambling."
—Ambrose Bierce (1842–1914), American writer

3. "Gambling: the sure way of getting nothing for something."
—Wilson Mizner (1876–1933), American dramatist

4. "No wife can endure a gambling husband–unless he is a steady winner."
—Lord Thomas Robert Dewar (1864–1930), British whiskey distiller

5. "Women's total instinct for gambling is satisfied by marriage."
—Gloria Steinem (1935–), American feminist and writer

6. "There is no gambling like politics."—Benjamin Disraeli (1804–1881), British prime minister and novelist

7. "Luck is not chance, it's toil. Fortune's expensive smile is earned."
—Emily Dickinson (1830–1886), American poet

8. "One must have the courage to dare."—Fedor Dostoevsky (1821–1881), Russian novelist and compulsive gambler

9. "The urge to gamble is so universal and its practice so pleasurable that I assume it must be evil."
—Heywood Braun (1888–1939), sports journalist

10. "I love blackjack, but I'm not addicted to gambling. I'm addicted to sitting in a semi circle."
—Mitch Hedberg (1968–2005), American comedian

11. "He was subject to a kind of disease, which at that time, they called lack of money."
—Francois Rabelais (1493–1553), French writer and physician

12. "Gambling promises the poor what property performs for the rich–something for nothing."
—George Bernard Shaw (1856–1950), Irish playwright

13. "Life is a gamble with terrible odds. If it were a bet, you would not take it."
—Tom Stoppard (1937–), British playwright

14. "God does not play dice with the universe."
—Albert Einstein (1879–1955), physicist

15. "I've got a 15-year-old son and a 10-year-old daughter, and if they were going to do one of the following things: be an alcoholic; be a drug offender; beat their wife or husband; or gamble, I hope they would gamble."
—Pete Rose (1941–), baseball player

ON YOUR OWN

Imagine that you just won $5,000 at a casino. Write a short postcard or note to a friend or relative describing what you will do in the next 24 hours.

....

....

....

....

....

....

....

"The heart has its reasons which
reason does not understand."

Blaise Pascal (1623–1662),
French philosopher

33

DO YOU MATCH?

REFLECTING

Who will you choose to share your life with? Are you considering marriage? Are you already married? Use these questions as a springboard to reflect on your options, choices, and desires.

1. Why do (did) you want to get married?

2. Do (did) you have a checklist of qualities for a potential spouse?

3. What are the three main qualifications on your checklist? Partner? Provider? Lover? Friend?

4. When did you fall in love? Did one person fall first? Who?

5. How did you know your lover was the one? How did your thinking evolve?

6. Did you ever have moments of doubt? How did your thinking evolve?

7. Do you think people should live together before they get married? Why? Can you share some examples?

8. Are sex, love and marriage linked in your mind, or is each separate? How are they different?

9. What are some endearing qualities of your companion?

10. Do you like your partner's friends? Do you respect them? Why?

11. What advice have your parents and close friends given you? Your extended family? How important is their opinion in your decision? Why?

12. Do you think you are marrying only an individual or are you also marrying your spouse's family? How would you describe your potential in-laws?

13. What does your partner do that annoys you?

14. Do you expect to be the pilot, co-pilot, or passenger in the marriage? Why?

15. What, if anything, would definitely cause you to divorce? Why?

VOCABULARY

Review these words and expressions. Circle the words that you know.

potential ....

neat freak ....

spouse ....

nupital ....

conflicts ....

checklist ....

resolve ....

pre-nuptial ....

compatible ....

pack rat ....

justify ....

evolve ....

PROVERBS

What do these proverbs mean? Can you share some other proverbs?

The needle is always accompanied by the thread.—Korean

Strange is the affinity that binds two in marriage.—Japanese

Whoever marries only for beauty will live in misery.—Russian

THE CONVERSATION CONTINUES...

1. Thinking about personal preferences, do you like to stay up late or get up early? Do you have compatible sleeping habits?

2. Do you have similar media habits? Do you have similar tastes in TV shows and movies?

3. Where do you prefer to live? Country? City? Farm? Apartment? House?

4. Are you a pack rat? Are you a neat freak? Are your styles compatible?

5. Will you still love your partner when he or she is 64? Will your partner love you with wrinkles?

6. Do you know an older couple that might be a model for a good partnership? Who are they?

7. What activities do you enjoy in your leisure time? Will your spouse join you?

8. Do you and your lover share spending philosophies? Do you shop together?

9. Do you expect to live with older generations? Who? Why? Where? When?

10. What is your approach to settling conflicts? How often do you have conflicts?

11. Do you want children? How many?

NOTES & QUESTIONS

....

....

....

....

....

....

....

....

12. Do you believe in birth control? Why?

13. What do you think your baby would look like? Why?

14. What kind of parent do you expect your spouse to become? Why?

15. Would you want your sons to be like the man you're marrying? Would you want your daughters to be like the woman you're marrying?

16. Do you expect to follow family or religious traditions? Which ones? Why?

17. If disagreements arise about children, how do you expect to resolve them?

18. Do you think all money should be shared or should each spouse have separate bank accounts? Why? How do you expect to manage household expenses?

19. What were the best gifts that you've given or received in the relationship?

20. What passions do you share? What unites you as a couple?

21. Do you have a favorite photograph of you as a couple? Can you describe it?

22. Where do you want to travel together? What do you want to see together?

23. What are you looking forward to doing together as a married couple?

24. How do you expect your life to change once you are married? What are some advantages of being married?

25. Do you have any tips or suggestions on how to create and preserve a happy marriage?

QUOTATIONS

Which two quotations come closest to your attitudes?

1. "By all means marry; if you get a good wife, you'll become happy; if you get a bad one, you'll become a philosopher."
—Socrates (470–339 B.C.E.), Greek philosopher

2. "Man's best possession is a sympathetic wife."
—Euripides (480–406 B.C.E.), playwright

3. "I'm so gullible. I'm so damn gullible. And I am so sick of being gullible."
—Lana Turner (1921–1995), Hollywood star married seven times

4. "Marriage is a great institution, but I'm not ready for an institution."
—Mae West (1892–1980), American actress

5. "Love means never having to say you're sorry."
—Ali McGraw in *Love Story* (1970)

6. "Love is the only sane and satisfactory answer to the problem of human existence."
—Erich Fromm (1900–1980), psychologist

"Love is the ideal thing, marriage a real thing; a confusion of the real with the ideal never goes unpunished."

Goethe (1749–1832),
German poet, novelist, and scientist

7. "Marriage: A word that should be pronounced 'mirage.'"
   —Herbert Spencer (1820–1903), English philosopher

8. "No matter who you get married to, you wake up married to somebody else."
   —Marlon Brando in *Guys and Dolls* (1955)

9. "Second marriage: the triumph of hope over experience."
   —Dr. Samuel Johnson (1709–1784), English writer

10. "Marriage is a very good thing, but I think it's a mistake to make a habit of it."
    —W. Somerset Maugham (1874–1965), English novelist

11. "A happy marriage is a long conversation that always seems too short."
    —Andre Maurois (1885–1967), French author

12. "A successful marriage is not a gift; it is an achievement."
    —Ann Landers (1918–2002), American advice columnist

1. ....
   • ....
   • ....

2. ....
   • ....
   • ....

3. ....
   • ....
   • ....

ON YOUR OWN

With your class partner, list three celebrity marriages that have ended in divorce. For each couple who divorced, list two reasons you think their marriage did not last.

Then, list three marriages of well-known people that have lasted more than 20 years. For each couple, list two reasons why you think their marriage lasted. Share with the class.

1. ....
   • ....
   • ....

2. ....
   • ....
   • ....

3. ....
   • ....
   • ....

34
HANDLING STRESS

SHARING TIPS

Sometimes we all feel stressed. Take turns asking and responding to these questions. Feel free to skip any awkward questions. Listen sympathetically.

1. What are common reasons for stress in people's personal lives?

2. Have you felt stress recently? Describe a recent stressful experience.

3. When is your workplace stressful?

4. Which school situations make you stressful at times?

5. Do you eat more or less when you're stressed? Do you have any special comfort foods?

6. Do you have stomach ulcers or high blood pressure?

7. Do your hands shake when you're stressed? Any other physical symptoms?

8. When you're stressed, are you fearful? Are you sad? Are you angry?

9. How do others know when you're stressed? Do you yell? Become silent?

10. Do you remember feeling stressed as a child? Why?

11. Do you feel more stress as an adult than you did as a child?

12. Do you know any "stress junkies" who thrive on pressure? What professions might attract these people? Why?

13. How can stress help you? Have you ever been inspired by stress?

14. Can stress be fun? Do you like horror movies? Do you like roller coasters? Are you a sports fan?

15. In what other situations does stress make you feel more alive?

16. Have you ever been to a spa or had a massage? Did it help you relieve stress?

17. What kind of music relaxes you and relieves stress?

18. Do you exercise or play sports to lessen your stress? How often? Does it help?

Please circle the words that you know. Ask your partner or teacher for the meanings of the other words.

stress ....

comfort..

spa ....

symptom ....

unhealthy ....

fan ....

relieve ....

adventuresome..

red-flag..

risks ....

thrive ....

strive ....

overcome..

PROVERBS

Pick your favorite and tell your partner when you would use it.

Go with the flow.—American

Worry often gives a small thing a big shadow.—Swedish

Look before you leap.—American

You can't catch the cubs without entering the tiger's den.—Korean

Time spent laughing is time spent with the gods.—Japanese

Smooth seas do not make skillful sailors.—English

THE CONVERSATION CONTINUES...

1. Do you want relaxation, adventure, or something else from your vacation?

2. Does shopping reduce stress for you or does it create stress for you?

3. Can you name three unhealthy ways that people use to reduce stress?

4. Can you name three healthy ways that people use to reduce stress?

5. In which ways has the technology in your life reduced your stress?

6. In which ways has the technology in your life increased your stress?

7. Do you think you are more or less stressed than your parents were when they were the age you are now? In what ways? Why?

8. What are potential risks for people who seem to thrive on stress?

9. How do you know when you're stressed? Do you have a red flag warning?

10. How have you overcome stressful situations? How do you handle daily stress?

REMEMBER...

Be open

Keep your perspective

Be supportive

11. What stress-busting tips can you suggest for others?

12. Would you enjoy a stress-free life? Is it a possibility?

QUOTATIONS

Please read the quotations below. Which ones make the most sense to you?

1. "There is no such thing as pure pleasure; some anxiety always goes with it."
   —Ovid (43 B.C.–18A.D.), poet

2. "A problem is a chance for you to do your best."
   —Duke Ellington (1890–1974), jazz composer and band leader

3. "The only thing we have to fear is fear itself."
   —Franklin Delano Roosevelt (1882–1945), 32nd U.S. President

4. "Facing it—always facing it—that's the way you get through. Face it!"
   —Joseph Conrad (1857–1924), Polish-born British novelist

5. "Don't sweat the small stuff, and it's all small stuff."
   —Dr. Richard Carlson (1956–), bestselling American author and psychologist

6. "The chief danger in life is that you may take too many precautions."
   —Dr. Alfred Adler (1870–1937), Austrian psychologist

7. "More than any time in history, mankind faces a crossroad: One path leads to despair and utter hopelessness; the other to total extinction. Let us pray we have the wisdom to choose correctly."
   —Woody Allen (1935–), American film director, actor, and comic

8. "Man needs difficulties; they are necessary for health."
   —Carl Gustav Jung (1875–1961), Swiss psychiatrist

9. "It was the best of times; it was the worst of times."
   —Charles Dickens (1812–1870), English novelist

10. "Do what you can, with what you have, where you are."
    —Theodore Roosevelt (1858–1919), 26th U. S. President

11. "I don't think of all the misery, but of the beauty that remains."
    —Anne Frank (1929–1945), writer

12. "With me, a change of trouble is as good as a vacation."
    —David Lloyd George (1863–1945), British prime minister during WWI

13. "In the depth of winter, I finally learned that within me there lay an invincible summer."
    —Albert Camus (1913–1960), French novelist

14. "An early morning walk is a blessing for the whole day."
    —Henry David Thoreau (1817–1862), writer

ON YOUR OWN

Find an article on dealing with stress. Prepare to share the information you found with your classmates in a small group.

You might also be asked to give a very short report to the class.

**"If I am not for myself,
who will be for me?
But if I am only for myself,
what am I?
And if not now, when?"**

HILLEL
(1st century CE), rabbi

> **"Whenever you are asked if you can do a job, tell 'em, 'Certainly, I can!'—and get busy and find out how to do it."**
>
> Theodore Roosevelt (1858–1919),
> cowboy, police chief, colonel,
> and 26th U.S. President

35

PRACTICING JOB INTERVIEWS

ANTICIPATING QUESTIONS

Work with your partner and role-play applying for a position in your field. Switch roles every ten questions. Use complete sentences.

1. Have you ever applied for a job with our organization before?

2. Have you ever worked in the United States before? Where?

3. Are you eligible to work in the U.S.? Can you provide documentation?

4. Have you ever worked off-the-books?

5. May we investigate your background? Can we run a credit check?

6. Have you ever been laid off? Have you ever been fired?

7. Have you ever been sued? Have you ever been arrested?

8. Have you ever been caught stealing? Stolen from your employer?

9. Have you ever been investigated for misconduct? Have you ever had a professional license revoked?

10. Have you ever taken a psychological test before?

11. Have you ever hidden problems from your managers?

12. Have you ever lied on a job application? Have you lied on your resume?

13. Have you ever taken a lie detector test? A drug test? A handwriting test? A psychological test?

14. Have you ever quit without giving two weeks notice?

15. Have you ever studied computers? Have you worked with computers before?

16. Have you ever used Microsoft Office? Other software? Which programs?

17. Have you ever used a cash register? Fax machine? Xerox machine?

18. What skills have you learned in your professional life?

VOCABULARY

Please circle the words that you know. Ask your partner or teacher for the meanings of the other words.

apply ....

applicant ....

background ....

resign ....

bonus ....

misconduct ....

software ....

revoke ....

client ....

promoted ....

SAYINGS

Read the common sayings and proverbs below. Can you add two more?

The secret of getting ahead is getting started.

Short answers save trouble.

What you don't ask, you don't get.

Anything worth having is worth working for.

(Add your own) ....

(Add your own) ....

THE CONVERSATION CONTINUES...

1. What did you learn from your last job? Best manager? Worst boss?

2. Have you ever been certified in a professional field? How did you prepare?

3. Have you ever been evaluated by a supervisor? What did you learn?

4. What suggestions have you made at work to help the company?

5. Were your suggestions adopted? Were the suggestions successful?

6. Have you ever been promoted? What was your new title?

7. Have you ever received a bonus? Have you ever gotten a raise?

8. Have you ever worked on commission? Have you ever worked as a salesperson?

9. Have you ever traveled out of town for work? What did you do?

10. Have you ever volunteered for overtime? Have you ever declined overtime?

11. Have you ever worked on the weekends? Week nights?

12. Have you ever worked 12-hour shifts? What shift is best for you?

13. Have you ever spoken English with customers or clients?

14. Have you ever worked as a mechanic/salesperson/researcher/ nurse before?

REMEMBER...

Be careful

Be honest

Be active

15. Have you ever taken care of young children? In America?

16. Do you prefer working alone or with others? Why?

17. What items have you sold? Did you sell merchandise in English?

18. Have you ever worked with difficult customers? What was your approach? Did it work?

19. Have you ever hired people? What did you look for in applicants?

20. Have you ever worked as a supervisor? Foreman? Manager?

21. What tips do you have for young people entering your profession?

22. Why should you be hired for this position?

QUOTATIONS

Read the quotations aloud to your partner. Which quotes do both of you agree with? Which quotation is your favorite? Why?

1. "The difference between a job and a career is the difference between 40 and 60 hours a week."—Robert Frost (1874–1963), poet

2. "You have to have your heart in the business and the business in your heart."—Thomas J. Watson (1874–1956), founder of IBM

3. "If you don't know where you are going, you will probably end up somewhere else."
—Dr. Laurence J. Peter (1919–1990), educator

4. "In a hierarchy every employee tends to rise to his level of incompetence."
—Dr. Laurence J. Peter (1919–1990), educator

5. "You may be disappointed if you fail, but you are doomed if you don't try."
—Beverly Sills (1929–2007), opera singer

6. "Luck is not something that you can mention in the presence of self-made men."
—E.B. White (1899–1985), American writer

7. "In business for yourself, not by yourself."
—Ray Kroc (1902–1984), McDonald's founder

8. My father taught me to work; he did not teach me to love it."
—Abraham Lincoln (1809–1865), 16th U.S. President

9. "I want to work for a company that contributes to and is part of a community. I want not just to invest in; I want to believe in."
—Anita Roddick (1943–2007), Body Shop founder

10. "The only place where success comes before work is in the dictionary."
—Vidal Sassoon (1928–), hair stylist and salon tycoon

11. "If you have to support yourself, you had bloody well better find some way that is going to be interesting. And you don't do that by sitting around."
—Katharine Hepburn (1907–2003), movie icon

12. "Success is 10 percent inspiration and 90 percent perspiration."
—Thomas A. Edison (1847–1931), American inventor

ON YOUR OWN

You have started a new business. How will you choose your employees? List the first seven steps you will take.

....

....

....

....

....

....

....

"Whether our work is art or science or the daily work of society, it is only the form in which we explore our experience which is different."

Jacob Bronowski
(1908–1974), scientist

36

WORK RELATIONSHIPS

SHARING STORIES

Most people have to work to survive. Some people love their work. What are your work experiences? How do others manage? Share your thoughts with your class partner. Remember to help each other.

1. Do you work? Are you retired?

2. Do you have a regular schedule? Which shift do you work?

3. Would you like more hours? Fewer hours? Why?

4. Which department do you work in? Do you have a title?

5. Do you work alone or with other staff members?

6. Can you describe a typical day at work?

7. Do you use a computer at work? What computer software programs do you use?

8. How do you use email or the Internet at work? When? Why?

9. Have computers changed your work habits in any way? How?

10. Do you have a high profile position? Are you visible at your job?

11. Is there a career ladder at your workplace?

12. How do you get along with your co-workers? Are you a team player? Do you enjoy the work atmosphere?

13. Do you socialize with your co-workers outside of work? Where do you go?

14. How does your company/school encourage networking among co-workers?

15. Does your company use interns or college students? How?

16. What qualities does your organization look for in new employees?

17. Have you ever had a mentor? Who? How did this person teach you the ropes at work?

18. Are you a mentor to anyone at work? What do you do to help?

VOCABULARY

Work with your partner to understand the meaning of each of the vocabulary words. Then, circle the ones that you're sure you know.

shift ....

title ....

retire ....

co-worker ....

profession ....

hire ....

fire ....

supervisor ....

supervise ....

mentor ....

ambition ....

manager ....

NOTES & QUESTIONS

....

....

....

....

....

....

....

....

PROVERBS

Have you heard any of these before? Circle the ones with which you agree.

Many hands make light work.—Latin

Cash in hand is better than credit to a rich customer.—Korean

Too many pilots are bound to sink the ship.—Chinese

All work and no play makes Jake a dull boy.—English

Time is money.—Greek

THE CONVERSATION CONTINUES...

1. Have you ever complained about a co-worker? A boss? How did they upset you?

2. How has a co-worker impressed you? What have you learned from your co-workers?

3. How is your profession shown in movies? Can you give an example?

4. What are some common misperceptions about your field? Example?

5. What qualities should a manager, director, or boss have in your field? Why?

6. What are some things a rude or obnoxious boss might do?

7. Have you ever had to deal with a rude, difficult, or crazy boss?

8. Who is the best manager, director, or boss you've ever had? Why?

9. Have you ever supervised someone? Were you a good manager? Why?

10. How would you describe your management style? Can you give an example?

11. Have you ever hired someone? What did you look for? Why?

12. Have you ever evaluated people at work? Have you had to fire someone? Why?

13. What makes someone a professional in your field? How can people stand out?

14. How do some people neglect their work duties because of family responsibilities?

15. Have you ever known someone to neglect their family because of their work?

16. What is a workaholic?

17. How would you describe your work habits?

18. How do you keep track of your tasks, meetings, and relationships at work?

19. Do you have any time management tips to share?

20. Do you think most Americans work to live or live to work? Why?

21. Have you recently updated your professional skills? How?

22. What are your professional ambitions? Why?

QUOTATIONS

With the help of your partner, read aloud each of the following quotations. Circle the ones with which both of you agree.

1. "Work keeps at bay three great evils: boredom, vice, and need."
   —Voltaire (1694–1778), French philosopher

2. "I'm a great believer in luck, and I find the harder I work the more of it I have."—Thomas Jefferson (1743–1826), U.S. President and the man on the nickel

3. "I don't like work–no man does–but I like what is in the work–The chance to find yourself."
   —Joseph Conrad (1857–1924), British novelist

4. "Competition brings out the best in products and the worst in people."—David Sarnoff (1881–1971), leader of RCA

5. "I don't meet competition; I crush it."
   —Charles Revson (1906–1975), founder of Revlon

6. "Where work is a pleasure, life is a joy! When work is a duty, life is slavery."
   —Maxim Gorky (1868–1936), Russian/Soviet novelist

7. "There are an enormous number of managers who have retired on the job."
   —Peter Drucker (1909–2005), American business guru

8. "There is no such thing as a free lunch."
   —Milton Friedman (1912–2006), economist

9. "Without work all life goes rotten."
   —Albert Camus (1913–1960), French writer

10. "I'm lazy. But it's lazy people who invented the wheel and the bicycle because they didn't like walking or carrying things."
    —Lech Walesa (1943–), Polish President and Labor leader

ON YOUR OWN

Choose a quote that relates to the job you have now or one you once had. In five sentences, tell the class how this quote relates to your work experience.

....

....

....

....

....

....

....

....

37

LEARNING IN SCHOOL

SHARING SCHOOL STORIES

We have spent thousands of hours in schools, learned many skills, and collected many stories. Share your school stories with a classmate.

1. When did you first go to school? Was it an urban, a rural, or a suburban school?

2. How did you usually get to school? Did you walk, take a bus, ride a bike or use another method?

3. How long was your commute to elementary school? High school?

4. How many students were usually in your class? What was the atmosphere like?

5. Do you remember the name of your elementary school? High school?

6. Did you attend a public or private school? Why?

7. Was there a school dress code? What were some other rules?

8. How would you describe your elementary school? Did you enjoy it?

9. Were your parents involved in your studies? How?

10. Were you given report cards? How often? What kind of grades did you get?

11. Can you describe the classroom conditions in your high school?

12. How large was your high school? What was the lunchroom like?

13. What subjects did you take in high school? Did you choose your courses?

14. What was your favorite course? Why?

15. Were there any classes that you dreaded or hated? Why?

16. Did you have to take any exams? Which exam was the most difficult? Why?

17. Was cheating common? Why? Did you ever cheat? How?

VOCABULARY

Circle the words that you know. Look up the other words.

adversity...

commute...

elementary...

dress code...

report cards...

tutor...

role model...

bully...

field trip...

mascot...

PROVERBS

Circle the ones with which you agree.

Learning colors a man more than the deepest dye.—Chinese

The dog near a school will learn
to recite lessons in three years.—Korean

He who is afraid to ask is ashamed of learning.—Danish

We learn to walk by stumbling.—Bulgarian

In time, even a bear can be taught to dance.—Yiddish

Don't step on your teacher's shadow.—Korean

THE CONVERSATION CONTINUES...

1. Have you ever had a tutor? Why?

2. Do you like to study alone or in groups? Why?

3. Do you remember taking field trips? Where did you go?

4. How many years of formal education have you had?

5. Do you remember any bullying or violent fights at school? Were guns used?

6. Were you given too much homework? Too little, or just enough?

7. What was your favorite place to study? Can you describe the area?

8. What are cram schools?

9. What after-school activities, clubs, or sports did you participate in?

10. What sports did the school compete in? Did they have a mascot? Cheerleaders?

11. What are you proud of doing in your academic studies? Did you win any awards?

12. What was your best school year? Or what did you enjoy most about school?

13. What's your earliest school memory? Favorite memory?

14. Who was your role model or mentor (teacher, coach) at school?

REMEMBER...

Explore

Take risks

Do your best

15. Have you kept in touch with anyone from your high school? Who? How?

16. Would you want your children to attend the schools that you attended? Why?

17. Can you compare and contrast schools in the United States and your native country?

18. Do you have any ideas on how to reform or improve schools?

QUOTATIONS

Pick your three favorite quotes and circle them. Discuss them.

1. "The world itself rests upon the breath of the children in our schools."
   —Talmud

2. "Only the educated are free."
   —Epictetus (55–135), Stoic philosopher

3. "The wise are instructed by reason, average minds by experience, the stupid by necessity and the brute by instinct."
   —Marcus Cicero (106–43 B.C.E.) statesman

4. "Education: The path from cocky ignorance to miserable uncertainty."
   —Mark Twain (1835–1910), American writer/humorist

5. "Nothing in life is to be feared. It is only to be understood."
   —Marie Curie (1867–1934), Physicist

6. "Education is helping the child realize his potentialities."
   —Erich Fromm (1900–1980), Psychoanalyst

7. "They know enough who know how to learn."
   —Henry Adams (1838–1918), historian

8. "Education is a progressive discovery of our own ignorance."
   —Will Durant (1885–1981), historian

9. "The highest result of education is tolerance."
   —Helen Keller (1880–1968), author

10. "My education was dismal. I went to a school for mentally disturbed teachers."
    —Woody Allen (1935–), American comedian

11. "America believes in education: the average professor earns more money in a year than a professional athlete earns in a whole week."
    —Evan Esar (1899–1995), humorist

12. "Education is a kind of continuing dialogue and a dialogue assumes, in the nature of the case, different points of view."
    —Robert Hutchins (1899–1977), educator

13. "Human history becomes more and more a race between education and catastrophe."
    —H.G. Wells (1866–1946), English novelist

14. "You know there is a problem with the education system when you realize that out of the 3 R's, only one begins with an R."
—Dennis Miller (1953–), American comedian

15. "A child miseducated is a child lost."
—John F. Kennedy (1917–1963), 35th U.S. President

16. "Perhaps the most valuable result of all education is the ability to make yourself do the thing you have to do, when it ought to be done, whether you like it or not."
—Thomas H. Huxley (1825–1895) scientist

17. "Education is the ability to listen to almost anything without losing your temper or your self-confidence."
—Robert Frost (1874–1963), poet

....
....
....
....
....
....
....
....
....
....
....
....
....
....

ON YOUR OWN
At left, write a paragraph about your favorite teacher in your homeland.

38

STUDYING ENGLISH

SHARING EXPERIENCES

English has emerged as the global tongue in the early 21st century. Yet, English remains a crazy, confusing, and misspelled language. Interview a classmate and share your joys and frustrations in learning this important language.

1. Where did you first hear English spoken?

2. Which English words have been adopted into your native language?

3. Where is English most commonly used in your native country? Why?

4. Do advertisements sometimes use English words? Why?

5. When did you first study English? Were you excited, bored, or indifferent?

6. How long have you studied English? What inspired you to study it? Where have you studied English?

7. Have you had any negative experiences learning English?

8. Are there English classes for adults in your country? Are they expensive?

9. What was the best English class you ever had? Why?

10. What method of learning seems to work best for you? Why?

11. Have you found an excellent tool for learning English? What?

12. Do you have a good bilingual dictionary? Can you bring it to class?

13. What's your favorite English word or expression?

14. Do you listen, speak, read, and write English every day?

15. Where do you usually speak English? Why?

16. What materials do you read in English? Why?

17. Do you speak English with American neighbors? Co-workers? Friends? Classmates?

VOCABULARY

Please circle the words that you know, and find out the meaning of the other words. Use several vocabulary words to write three questions.

adopt...

inspire..

bilingual...

audiobook...

monolingual..

eavesdrop...

subtitle...

examiner...

closed-caption...

exclusive..

inclusive...

offer...

THE CONVERSATION CONTINUES...

1. Have you ever called a 1-800-number just to practice your English? What happened?

2. Have you ever listened to an audio book? Which one? Was it enjoyable? Did you learn many new words?

3. Do you ever eavesdrop, or just listen intently, to conversations around you?

4. Do you listen to the radio? Do you have some favorite shows? Why?

5. Do you watch American movies with subtitles? Why?

6. Do you use the closed-captioning feature on many TV programs? Why?

7. Is it easier to spell in English than in your best language? Why?

8. What are some positive aspects of the English language?

9. What are some characteristics that make learning English difficult?

10. Do you have a driver's license? Did you take the exam in English? Why?

11. Should all government agencies exclusively use English? Why or why not?

12. Are you a U.S. citizen? What questions did the examiner ask you?

13. If you were designing the citizenship test, would you change anything? What?

14. What would you not feel comfortable doing in English now?

15. Where would you like to feel more comfortable speaking English?

16. In your opinion, why has English become more popular in the last 20 years?

17. What tips can you offer friends who want to improve their English?

QUOTATIONS

Read aloud all the quotations. Pick your favorites and discuss.

1. "I speak two languages, Body and English."
   —Mae West (1892–1980), actress

2. "'I am' is reportedly the shortest sentence in the English language. Could it be that 'I do' is the longest sentence?"
   —George Carlin (1937–), American comedian

3. "Every immigrant who comes here should be required within five years to learn English or leave the country."
   —Theodore Roosevelt (1858–1919), 26th U.S. President

4. "Even if you do learn to speak correct English, whom are you going to speak it to?"
   —Clarence Darrow (1857–1938), American lawyer

5. "England and America are two countries divided by a common language."
   —George Bernard Shaw (1856–1950), Irish playwright, Nobel Prize winner

6. "Next to money, English is the leading international language."
   —Evan Esar (1899–1995), American humorist

7. "'Check enclosed' are the most beautiful words in English."
   —Dorothy Parker (1893–1967), American writer

8. "The most beautiful words in the English language are 'not guilty.'"
   —Maxim Gorky (1868–1936), Russian novelist

9. "The most terrifying words in the English language are: 'I'm from the government and I'm here to help you.'"
   —Ronald Reagan (1911–2004), 40th U.S. President

10. "There is no such thing as 'The Queen's English.' The property has gone into the hands of a joint stock company and we own the bulk of the stock."—Mark Twain (1835–1910), writer

11. "Slang is a language that rolls up its sleeves, spits on the its hands, and goes to work."—Carl Sandburg (1878–1967), American poet, Folklorist, and historian

12. "Words are, of course, the most powerful drug used by mankind."
    —Rudyard Kipling (1865–1936), British author and Nobel laureate

13. "In this country, it doesn't make any difference where you were born. It doesn't make any difference who your parents were. It doesn't make any difference if, like me, you couldn't even speak English until you were in your twenties."—Arnold Schwarzenegger (1947–), California Governor and American actor

14. "Apparently Arnold was inspired by President Bush, who proved you can be a successful politician in this country even if English is your second language."
    —Conan O'Brien (1963–), American talk show host

15. "Fatherhood is helping your children learn English as a foreign language."
    —Bill Cosby (1937–), American comedian and actor

ON YOUR OWN

Using only English words, write a favorite food or dish next to each letter. For example: E, Eggs.

E..

N..

G..

L ....

I ....

S ....

H..

39
COMING TO AMERICA

REFLECTIONS

How far have you traveled to come to the United States? Share your experiences and learn more about your classmates during this conversation.

1. What's your native country? How long did you live there?

2. Are there many immigrants from your native country? Why?

3. Are there certain areas where immigrants from your country often live?

4. What makes your state attractive to new immigrants?

5. How long have you been in the United States?

6. Who are some famous refugees who found safety and success in the U.S.?

7. Can you think of prominent Asian immigrants? Russian? European? Hispanic?

8. Can you identify some successful immigrant artists, filmmakers, or musicians?

9. What are some ways that immigrants have contributed to the American economy?

10. How does an immigrant become a citizen in your native country?

11. What are some legal differences between citizens, guest workers, and illegal immigrants in your country of origin?

12. In your homeland, how old do you have to be to drink alcohol? Buy it? In the U.S.?

13. What differences have you noticed in driving habits or traffic laws?

14. When do bars/clubs usually close there? Do you think American bars close early?

15. Do many people like to smoke at work in your native country? Can children buy cigarettes there?

VOCABULARY

Please circle the words that you know. Ask your partner or teacher for the meanings of the other words.

tradition ....

taboo ....

refugee ....

immigrant ....

passport ....

consent ....

allegiance ....

requirement ....

prominent citizen..

forbidden ....

consequence..

citizenship ....

melting pot ....

naturalized ....

PROVERBS

REMEMBER...

Explore

Be curious

Take risks

Read these common sayings and proverbs. Can you add two more?

Anything can happen.

Only in America.

(Add another)..

(Add another)..

THE CONVERSATION CONTINUES...

1. Is gambling popular in your native country? Is it legal? Where?

2. Is spanking your child legal? Can teachers spank or "tap" children?

3. Do children have to attend school? Do they have to wear uniforms?

4. At what age may people marry? What's the age of consent in your native country?

5. Can you compare the laws about marriage, divorce, and raising children?

6. What about guns? Are there any differences? Who can buy guns?

7. Can you compare the laws for violent criminals? What about capital punishment?

8. What are some common crimes in your native country? The U.S.?

9. Can you think of any silly or bad laws there? Here?

10. Can you think of some smart or good laws there? Here?

11. What are other differences between laws in your country and here?

12. Have you read or seen any negative consequences of this law? Can you give an example?

13. What are some taboos in your native country? What is socially forbidden? Why?

14. What are traditions do you appreciate from your native country?

15. What traditions or values do you hope your children will keep? Why?

16. How do traditions change? Can you give an example?

17. What American traditions do you like or want to adopt? Why?

18. Do you see America as more of a melting pot or a salad? Why?

19. What are some benefits of American citizenship? Disadvantages?

20. What are the citizenship requirements? What do you think they should be? Why?

21. Are you an American citizen? Do you plan to become one? Why?

QUOTATIONS

Read each quotation aloud, pick your favorites, and discuss them with your group.

1. "The bosom of America is open to receive not only the opulent and respectable stranger, but the oppressed and persecuted of all nations and religions."—George Washington (1732–1799), First President of the United States

2. "The mission of the United States is one of benevolent assimilation."—William McKinley (1843–1901), 25th U.S. President

3. "Old or young, healthy as a horse or a person with a disability that hasn't kept you down, man or woman, Native American, native born, immigrant, straight or gay–whatever; the test ought to be I believe in the Constitution, the Bill of Rights, and the Declaration of Independence. I believe in religious liberty. I believe in freedom of speech. I believe in working hard and playing by the rules. That ought to be the test."—Bill Clinton (1946–), 42nd U.S. President

4. "Americanism is a question of principle, of idealism, of character: it is not a matter of birthplace or creed or line of descent."—Theodore Roosevelt (1858–1919), 26th U.S. President

5. "God bless America, Land that I love. Stand beside her, and guide her, Through the night with a light from above."—Irving Berlin (1888–1989), composer

6. "America is God's Crucible, the great Melting-Pot where all the races of Europe are melting and reforming!"—Israel Zangwill (1864–1926), playwright who wrote *The Melting Pot*

7. "Throw your dreams into space like a kite, and you do not know what it will bring back, a new life, a new friend, a new love, or a new country."—Anaïs Nin, (1903–1977), writer

8. "And so, my fellow Americans: ask not what your country can do for you–ask what you can do for your country."—John F. Kennedy (1917–1963), 35th U.S. President

9. "I came over here as an immigrant, and what gave me the opportunities, what made me, is the open arms of Americans. I have been received. I have been adopted by America."—Arnold Schwarzenegger (1947–), California governor

ON YOUR OWN

What advice would you give a new immigrant or international student about he United States?

Write a short essay, and share your thoughts with your classmates.

40

EXPLORING AMERICAN CULTURE

EXPLORING

Blue jeans, cars, credit cards, elections, immigrants, juries, and jazz
have helped create American civilization. Chat with your partner about
America's diverse, dynamic culture.

1. Where were you born? How many miles, approximately, is your
   birthplace from here?

2. When did you arrive in the United States for the first time? How did
   you feel?

3. What were some of your first, or early, impressions? Why?

4. What has surprised you about living in the United States? Why?

5. Does your native country import anything from the United States?
   What?

6. Does your native country export to the United States? What?

7. What products, if any, seem exceptionally "American" to you? Why?

8. Which companies seem particularly American to you? Why?

9. Can you compare shopping here and in your native country?

10. Do any clothes seem "real" American to you? Blue jeans?
    Hawaiian shirts? Other?

11. Are American movies popular in your native country? Which
    kind? Why?

12. What types of music first developed in America?

13. Which Americans are popular in your native country now? Why?

14. Can you think of some Americans who are unpopular in your
    country? Why?

15. Has the United States changed its borders since 1776? How?

16. Has the population in the United States changed in the last 50
    years? How?

17. How many languages have you heard spoken in the United States?

VOCABULARY

With your partner, write definitions for the following words.

pursuit...

inalienable..

import...

individualism ....

export..

slogan..

freedom..

conformity ....

hero...

villain...

Bill of Rights...

popularity...

SLOGANS

Can you think of other state or national slogans? Add them to the list.

In God we trust.

Freedom is not free.

E pluribus unum (From many, one)

THE CONVERSATION CONTINUES...

1. What are some national symbols of the United States?

2. Can you think of some beautiful places in the United States?

3. Do you think America's geography has helped shaped its culture? How?

4. How many states are there in the United States? How many have you seen?

5. Have you visited Florida? Hawaii? New York? Nevada? Texas? Indiana?

6. What are some tourist attractions in Washington D.C.?

7. Do you agree that "America is a car culture"? Disagree? Why?

8. Where else would you like to go in the United States? Why?

9. Who are some important heroes in the U.S.? Why?

10. Who are some villains in American history or culture? Why?

11. What should Americans be proud of? Why?

12. What has disappointed you about living in the United States?

13. What American customs or laws do you appreciate? Which do you find strange?

14. What is the Bill of Rights? What freedoms does it protect?

15. What are some important phrases or slogans in the United States?

16. Why do you think so many immigrants move to the United States?

17. If you could change one thing about the U.S., what would it be?

18. What do you appreciate about American culture? Why?

19. What is *your* American dream? Why?

QUOTATIONS

Read aloud all the quotations. Circle three quotes and discuss.

1. "America is great because America is good, and if America ever ceases to be good, America will cease to be great."
   —Alexis De Tocqueville (1805–1859), historian

2. "The last hope of human liberty in this world rests on us."
   —Thomas Jefferson (1743–1826), U.S. President and statesman

3. "America is best described by one word, freedom."—Dwight D. Eisenhower (1890–1969) 34th U.S. President and General

4. "America is a place where Jewish merchants sell Zen love beads to agnostics for Christmas."
   —John Burton Brimer, design and garden writer

5. "America is the country where you buy a lifetime supply of aspirin for one dollar, and use it up in two weeks."
   —John Barrymore (1882–1942) actor

6. "America, which has the most glorious present still existing in the world today, hardly stops to enjoy it, in her insatiable appetite for the future."—Anne Morrow Lindbergh (1906–2001), author

7. "This is still a very wealthy country. The failure is of spirit and insight."
   —Jerry Brown (1938–) California Governor

8. "America is a land where a citizen will cross the ocean to fight for democracy–and won't cross the street to vote in a national election."
   —Bill Vaughan (1915–1977), writer

9. "My definition of a free society is a society where it is safe to be unpopular."
   —Adlai Stevenson (1900–1965), US ambassador to the UN

10. "The price of freedom of religion or speech or of the press is that we must put up with...a good deal of rubbish."
    —Robert H. Jackson (1892–1954), Supreme Court Justice

11. "Double–no triple–our troubles and we'd still be better off than any other people on earth."
    —Ronald Reagan (1911–2004), 40th U.S. President

12. "In one generation we have moved from denying a black man service at a lunch counter to elevating one to the highest military office in the country, and to being a serious contender for the presidency. This is a magnificent country and I am proud to be one of its sons."
    —Colin Powell (1937–), 65th U.S. Secretary of State

13. "The function of freedom is to free somebody else."
    —Toni Morrison (1937–) author, Nobel Prize winner in Literature

ON YOUR OWN

List five adjectives which you think describe American culture. Prepare to share your choices with your classmates.

1. ....

2. ....

3. ....

4. ....

5. ....

41
EXPLORING CITIES

SHARING STORIES

Cities are exciting. What adventures have you had in cities? Share your experiences with your classmate.

1. What is your native country? Where were you born?

2. What is the capital of your native country? Have you been there?

3. What interesting things are there to see or do in the capital city of your homeland? Where would you recommend tourists visit? Why?

4. Does that capital city have a mass transportation system ? Describe it.

5. Are the buses or subways punctual? Safe? Popular? Do you recommend a taxi?

6. Are there other major cities in your native country? Which do you prefer? Why?

7. What are the streets like in your hometown? Can people hear their own footsteps when they walk?

8. Do people walk more in your hometown than they do in the U.S.?

9. Are the streets and sidewalks more crowded in your hometown than they are here? Is the nightlife different? How?

10. Which cities have you lived in? How long did you live there?

11. Which cities have you visited as a tourist? When?

12. What do you like to do when you visit a new city?

13. What is the capital of the United States? Have you been there?

14. What are some famous landmarks in Washington, D.C.?

15. Which city in the United States has the largest population?

16. Can you name some famous spots in New York City? Neighborhoods?

17. Have you ever ridden on a subway? Where? What was it like?

18. Have you ever seen graffiti on city walls or subways? Was it attractive?

Circle three words you know. Write a sentence for each one.

attraction...

hometown...

skyscraper ....

landmark...

subway ....

graffiti...

slum...

capital...

ghetto ....

zoning ....

THE CONVERSATION CONTINUES...

REMEMBER...

Be alert

Make good mistakes

Be tolerant

1. Have you ever ridden in a taxi? Did you have a conversation with the driver?

2. Which American cities would you like to visit that you haven't seen yet? What attracts you?

3. What makes a good city? A great city? What makes a bad city?

4. What is a skyscraper? Do you like skyscrapers? Why?

5. What are some neighborhoods in your city? What makes them different?

6. What are some of the advantages of living near other people from your native country?

7. Are there any disadvantages to living near others from your homeland?

8. What are some dangers of urban living? Which films show those risks? Have you ever felt at risk in a city?

9. Do you feel safer living here or do you feel safer in your hometown? Why?

10. What is a ghetto? Are there many slums in your country? Where?

11. Do you enjoy museums? What kind? Which is your favorite urban museum?

12. What are some benefits to raising children in a city?

13. Can you describe your downtown? Is your downtown better in the day or night? Why?

14. What are some advantages to city life? What are some disadvantages?

15. Why do you think so many people are moving to cities?

16. If you could live anywhere in the world, where would you choose to live? Why?

QUOTATIONS

With your class partner, read aloud each of the quotations. Circle the three quotations which best express your feelings about cities.

1. "Rome wasn't built in a day."—Popular expression in ancient Rome

2. "City life: millions of people being lonesome together."
   —Henry David Thoreau (1817–1862), American writer

3. "I like a lot of things about the city, but I prefer the country because I don't have to wear a tie there."
   —Alexander Calder (1898–1976), American sculptor and artist

4. "If you would be known, and not know, vegetate in a village; if you would know, and not be known, live in a city."
   —Charles Colton (1780–1832), English clergyman

5. "What you want is to have a city which everyone…can admire as being something finer and more beautiful than he had ever dreamed of before…"
   —James Bryce (1838–1922), American architect

6. "A hick town is where there is no place to go where you shouldn't be."
   —Robert Quillen (1887–1948), Journalist

7. "Vulgar of manner, overfed, Overdressed and underbred; Heartless, Godless, hell's delight, Rude by day and lewd by night."
   —Byron Rufus Newton (1861–1938), "Owed to New York"

8. "Paris is a city of gaieties and pleasures where four-fifths of the inhabitants die of grief."
   —Nicholas Chamfort (1741–1794), French writer and wit

9. "The larger our great cities grow, the more irresistible becomes the attraction which they exert on the children of the country, who are fascinated by them, as the birds are fascinated by the lighthouse or the moths by the candle."
   —Havelock Ellis (1859–1939), British psychologist

10. "Los Angeles: Seventy-two suburbs in search of a city."
    —Dorothy Parker (1893–1967), American writer

11. "Los Angeles is a city no worse than others, a city rich and vigorous and full of pride, a city lost and beaten and full of emptiness."
    —Raymond Chandler (1888–1959), American author of crime stories

12. "A city is a place where there is no need to wait for next week to get the answer to a question, to taste the food of any country, to find new voices to listen to and familiar ones to listen to again."
    —Margaret Mead (1901–1978), anthropologist

13. "I'd rather wake up in the middle of nowhere than in any city on earth."
    —Steve McQueen (1930–1980), actor

14. "The city is a human zoo, not a concrete jungle."
    —Dr. Desmond Morris (1928–), zoologist

ON YOUR OWN

With a class group, list 10 American cities which you have heard about. Then, list 10 cities in other countries.

For each city, write two words or phrases which describe your association with that city. Example: New York–noisy, exciting.

Prepare a two-minute oral report on one of your visits to another city.

42

DRIVING CARS

TALKING

Pick and choose from the questions, and respond to your partner's comments.

1. How much time do you spend a week in cars? Why?

2. Do you have a state drivers' license? Did you take it in English?

3. Where do you usually drive? Do you drive during rush hour? Off-hours?

4. How long is your commute to work or school? How is the traffic?

5. Do you drive a car for your work? How many miles do you drive a year?

6. When did you start driving? Who taught you how to drive?

7. Where did you learn to drive? How long did it take? Was learning hard?

8. What is the age requirement to legally drive in your native country?

9. Is driving in the U.S. different from driving in your country? How?

10. Do your parents drive? When did they get their first car? Do you remember it?

11. When did you get your first car? Can you describe it?

12. How old do you think one should be to drive? Why?

13. Have you ever bought a car? How did you choose it?

14. What suggestions do you have for buying a used car?

15. Do you enjoy driving? How do you feel when you drive? Relaxed? Nervous?

16. How can you tell if somebody is a good driver? Are you one?

17. Have you ever gotten a traffic ticket? How did it happen?

18. Do you prefer driving on side streets, main roads, or the freeways? What are your reasons?

VOCABULARY

Do you and your partner know these words? Circle the words you know.

commute ....

carpool ....

traffic ....

rush hour ....

seat belt ....

tune-up ....

MPG ....

traffic ticket ....

lane ....

freeway ....

mandate ....

essential ....

SAYINGS

What do these expressions mean? Work with your partner and take a guess. Circle the ones you've heard before.

Better safe than sorry.

Buckle up.

Don't drink and drive.

Drive like hell and you'll get there.

Don't drive as if you owned the road. Drive as if you owned the car.

To get back on your feet, miss two car payments.

THE CONVERSATION CONTINUES...

1. Do you prefer to drive in the city or the country? Flat or hills?
2. Do you like long drives? Where do you like to go? Have you driven a scenic highway? Where?
3. What do you listen to when you drive? Music? News? Audiobooks?
4. Do you drive alone or in a carpool? What are some advantages of your style?
5. Do you drive an automatic or stick shift? Which do you prefer?
6. Have you ever driven anything other than a car? Truck? Motorcycle?
7. Do you own a car? Rent? Lease? What's the difference, anyway?
8. How can you find out your average miles per gallon? What's your MPG? Why does this matter to many drivers?
9. What is your biggest pet peeve about driving or other drivers?
10. When do you drive fast? When do you tend to drive slower? Why?
11. What is the longest distance you have ever driven? Did you drive alone?
12. What are some safety tips for drivers? Why do some state laws mandate wearing seat belts?

13. How often do you get a tune-up? Where do you usually go? Why?

14. Do you enjoy working on or repairing cars? What can you fix on a car?

15. Some people consider a car essential. Do you agree? Disagree? Why?

16. Have you ever been in a car accident? What happened? Were you injured?

17. What tips for safe driving can you share?

18. What are some positive aspects of America's car culture?

19. What's your favorite car? Do you have a fantasy car that you would love to own?

QUOTATIONS

Work in groups of three to read these quotes. Circle your favorite ones.

1. "Any customer can have a car painted any color that he wants so long as it is black."
   —Henry Ford (1863–1947), founder of Ford Motor Company

2. "The best car safety device is a rear-view mirror."
   —Dudley Moore (1935–2002), actor

3. "If GM had kept up with technology like the computer industry has, we would all be driving $25 cars that got 1,000 MPG."
   —Bill Gates (1955–), Microsoft founder

4. "Modern man drives a mortgaged car over a bond-financed highway on credit card gas."
   —Earl Wilson (1907–1987), newspaper columnist

5. "I have a BMW. But only because it stands for Bob Marley and the Wailers, and not because I need an expensive car."
   —Bob Marley (1945–1981), reggae star

6. "Mass transportation is doomed in North America because a person's car is the only place where he can be alone and think."
   —Marshall McLuhan (1911–1980), communications scholar

7. "Never have more children than you have car windows."
   —Erma Bombeck (1927–1996), humorist

8. "A car is useless in New York, essential everywhere else. The same with good manners."
   —Mignon McLaughlin (1913–1983), journalist

9. "I have bad reflexes. I was once run over by a car being pushed by two guys."
   —Woody Allen (1935–), comedian and film director

10. "Get your kicks on Route 66."
    —Title of a Nat King Cole hit song

11. "Thanks to the Interstate Highway System, it is now possible to travel across the country from coast to coast without seeing anything."
    —Charles Kuralt (1934–1997), broadcast journalist

12. "Standing in the middle of the road is very dangerous; you get knocked down by the traffic from both sides."
    —Margaret Thatcher (1925–), British Prime Minister

ON YOUR OWN

Look at ads, articles, or websites about a type of car, SUV, or truck that you might purchase in the future.

You might also want to clip a picture. Research the vehicle's features, ratings, and cost.

Give a short presentation on your research.

"He who does not prevent a crime when he can, encourages it."

Seneca (5 B.C.E.–65 A.D.),
Roman statesman

43

CRIME AND PUNISHMENT

EXCHANGING VIEWS

With a class partner, share your experiences and ideas about the problems of crime. Remember to be patient and encouraging with each other.

1. What do you consider minor crimes?

2. What are some terrible crimes?

3. Can you think of something that was illegal in your native country and is legal here?

4. What is legal in your country of birth that is illegal in the U.S?

5. Why are some cities using hidden cameras at stoplights? What is your reaction?

6. What crimes are commonly punished by a fine? Are these misdemeanors in your state?

7. In the United States, which crimes lead to jail time? Are these all felonies in your state?

8. What is capital punishment? Does your native country also have a death penalty? If so, for which crimes?

9. Do you feel safer where you live now or in your hometown? Why?

10. Where is the safest place you ever lived? What made the area so safe?

11. Have you ever walked in a risky area? What made the area feel dangerous?

12. How can you tell if a neighborhood has a high crime rate? What do you look for?

13. Do you have any friends in law enforcement? What do they do?

14. What are some situations for which you would call the police?

15. Have you ever seen, or witnessed, a crime? What happened?

16. Do you know anybody who has been robbed? Scammed? Burglarized?

Circle the words that you know.

misdemeanor ....

felony..

crime ....

criminal...

white collar ....

street crime ....

victimless..

mugged ....

scam ....

bribe ....

PROVERBS

Explain the meaning of one of the following proverbs to your partner.

Avarice goes before destruction.—Korean

All criminals turn preachers under the gallows.—Italian

If you are poor, don't cheat; if you are rich, don't presume.—Chinese

REMEMBER...

Watch your step

Keep perspective

Be honest

THE CONVERSATION CONTINUES...

1. Can you think of some situations in which a crime has been committed, but you would not call the police?

2. Are there differences between how the police behave here and in your native country?

3. What are some so-called "victimless" crimes? How can illegal drugs, smuggling, and prostitution be reduced?

4. What are some "white collar" crimes? Are bribery, identity theft, and fraud common?

5. What do you think the punishment for these felonies ought to be?

6. Have you watched the TV show "Law and Order"? "The Sopranos"? "CSI"? "The Wire"? Have you seen any older shows like "NYPD Blue"? "Columbo"? "Perry Mason"?

7. Do you enjoy police or detective shows on TV? Which ones?

8. Do you agree with critics who say TV creates more crime? Why?

9. How did your native country try to maintain public safety? Was it successful?

10. Can you list three ideas for improving public security?

11. Do you have any suggestions for reducing the danger of terrorism?

12. What is the difference between investigating and snooping?

13. Which American law, if any, would you change? Why?

14. Do you think there is more crime and violence today than 50 years ago? Why?

15. Can you share five suggestions for personal safety?

16. Why do you think the U.S. crime rate has dropped in the last decade?

QUOTATIONS

Read all the quotations. Then, re-read 1, 2, 3, 4, 5, 13, and 14. For each of these quotations, write agree or disagree. Share your answers with your partner.

1. "The greater the number of laws and enactments, the more thieves and robbers."
   —Lao-tzu (604–531 B.C.E.), Chinese philosopher

2. "The more corrupt the state, the more numerous the laws."
   —Tacitus (55–130), Roman philosopher

3. "Children are innocent and love justice, while most adults are wicked and prefer mercy."
   —G.K. Chesterton (1874–1936), English novelist and critic

4. "You can get much farther with a kind word and a gun than you can with a kind word alone."
   —Al Capone (1899–1947), Chicago gangster

5. "He didn't know the right people. That's all a police record means."
   —Raymond Chandler (1888–1959), American detective novelist

6. "Poverty may be the mother of crime, but lack of good sense is the father."—Jean de la Bruyere (1645–1696), French satiric writer

7. "The law, in its majestic equality, forbids the rich as well as the poor to sleep under the bridge, to beg in the streets, and to steal bread."
   —Anatole France (1844–1924), French writer and Nobel Prize winner in Literature

8. "Only crime and the criminal confront us with perplexity of radical evil."—Hannan Arendt (1906–1975), American philosopher

9. "Punishment is not for revenge, but to lessen crime and reform the criminal."—Elizabeth Fry (1780–1845), prison reformer

10. "There's a simple way to solve the crime problem: obey the law; punish those who do not."
    —Rush Limbaugh (1951–), American radio show host

11. "We don't seem to be able to check crime, so why not legalize it and then tax it out of business?"
    —Will Rogers (1879–1935), American folk hero

12. "Seeing a murder on television can help work off one's antagonisms. And if you haven't any antagonisms, the commercials will give you some."—Alfred Hitchcock (1899–1980), British film director

13. "Prisons don't rehabilitate, they don't punish, they don't protect, so what the hell do they do?"
    —Jerry Brown (1938–), California Governor and Attorney General

14. "Too much mercy…often resulted in further crimes which were fatal to innocent victims who need not have been victims if justice had been put first and mercy second."
    —Agatha Christie (1890–1976), English detective writer

ON YOUR OWN

How many English words of three or more letters can you make from the letters in CRIME and PUNISHMENT?

You may use a letter only as often for each word as it appears in these two words combined. Examples: mine, cup.

....

....

....

....

....

....

....

....

VOTING

SHARING VIEWS

Voting and having your vote count remain rare privileges around the world. Discuss elections and issues with your partner.

1. Have you voted in an election? When?

2. Does your native country have elections? How often?

3. How many parties usually participate in the elections?

4. What are the main national parties? What are some differences?

5. Have you ever been a member of a political party? Which? Why?

6. Who can vote in your country? Have the voting laws changed in your lifetime?

7. Can women vote? What's the minimum age?
   Can religious minorities vote?

8. How does someone become a citizen in your country?

9. What day of the week are national elections held?
   Can you cast an absentee vote?

10. Where do people physically vote? How do voters mark their ballots?

11. Do the candidates campaign? How?

12. Do the candidates hold televised debates? Who asks the questions?

13. Can you recall any political ads from a campaign?

14. What were some important issues in the last election?

15. Who won the last election? Was it a fair election? Why?

16. Have there ever been debates over the election results? Why?

17. What are the main political parties in the United States?

18. Can you compare and contrast elections here with those in your native country?

19. Who is eligible to vote in American elections? Are you eligible?

VOCABULARY

Please circle the words that you know. Write three questions using these words.

candidate ....

absentee ....

campaign ....

debates ....

contrast ....

election ....

eligible ....

naturalized ....

recall..

referendum ....

apathy ....

polls ....

SAYINGS

Read the common sayings and proverbs below. Can you add two more?

To the victor belong the spoils.

The squeaky wheel gets the grease.

Stand up and be counted.

A week is a long time in politics.

(Add your own) ....

(Add your own) ....

THE CONVERSATION CONTINUES...

1. Have you ever voted in an American election?

2. What are some advantages to the American system? Disadvantages?

3. What are referendums or initiatives? Can citizens in your state vote directly on reforms?

4. What is a public bond? What do government bonds finance?

5. Do voters have the right to recall public officials in your state?

6. What makes an effective or strong candidate? Why?

7. Who is the President? Who is the Vice President?
   To what party do they belong?

8. Who are your state's two Senators? Who is your Congressional Representative?

9. Who is the governor of your state? The mayor of your city?

10. What are some qualities you look for in elected officials? Why?

11. Who are some significant political leaders in the world today?
    Why did you select those leaders?

REMEMBER...

Be active

Ask good questions

Be tolerant

ON YOUR OWN

Create five campaign slogans for a candidate or cause of your choice.

1. ....

2. ....

3. ....

4. ....

5. ....

12. What are the advantages of being a naturalized citizen?

13. What are some important issues in your state right now? Why?

14. What are some local issues in your neighborhood or city? Why?

15. What do you think are some important national issues? Why?

16. What is apathy? Why is apathy so common among voters?

17. How could the election system be improved?

18. Do you expect to vote in the next election? Why?

QUOTATIONS

Circle quotes that you like. Which quotation is your favorite?

1. "Always do the right thing. This will gratify some and astonish the rest."—Mark Twain (1835–1910), American humorist

2. "…government of the people, by the people, for the people shall not perish from the earth."
—Abraham Lincoln (1809–1865), 16th U.S. President

3. "This woman's place is in the House–the House of Representatives."—Bella Abzug (1920–1998), American Congresswomen and feminist

4. "The only thing necessary for the triumph of evil is for good men to do nothing."—Edmund Burke (1729–1797), English statesman

5. "Sometimes it is said that man cannot be trusted with the government of himself. Can he, then, be trusted with the government of others?"
—Thomas Jefferson (1743–1826), U.S. President

6. "Where annual elections end, there slavery begins."
—John Adams (1735–1826), 2nd U.S. President

7. "Elections are won by men and women chiefly because most people vote against somebody rather than for somebody."
—Franklin Pierce Adams (1881–1960), journalist

8. "If the Republicans will stop telling lies about the Democrats, we will stop telling the truth about them."
—Adlai Stevenson (1900–1965), American statesman

9. "I belong to no organized political party–I am a Democrat."
—Will Rogers (1879–1935), American humorist and columnist

10. "I would rather be right than be President."
—Henry Clay (1777–1852), U.S. politician

11. "Democracy is the worst system devised by the wit of man except for all the others."
—Winston Churchill (1874–1965), British Prime Minister

12. "An election cannot give a country a firm sense of direction if it has two or more national parties which merely have different names, but are as alike in their principles and aims as two peas in the same pod."—Franklin D. Roosevelt (1882–1945), 32nd U.S. President; elected four times

13. "The happy ending is our national belief."
—Mary McCarthy (1912–1989), American novelist and critic

45

SEARCHING FOR HEROES

EXCHANGING IDEAS

In all countries and all times, people have had heroes. Who are yours?
Chat with your class partner about heroes.

1. Who are some heroes in cartoons or movies?

2. Do you have a favorite film hero? Who? Why?

3. Who are some classic heroes and heroines in literature?

4. Who are some traditional heroes in your native country? What did they do?

5. What is the difference between a hero and a role model?

6. What's the difference between a hero and a star?

7. Can you name someone who is a star and not a hero? Who?

8. What is the difference between a hero and an idol?

9. Can you name someone who has been idolized, but is not a hero?

10. What is the difference between a celebrity and a hero?

11. Must one be brave to be a hero? Can you think of an exception?

12. Are all brave people heroes? Why do you say that?

13. Do heroes have to be virtuous? Can you think of an exception?

14. Who are some heroes with flaws? Do all heroes have flaws?

15. Do heroes always sacrifice for others? If so, can you think of an exception?

16. Must one do something physical to be a hero? Can you think of an exception?

17. Is everyone who performs an outstanding physical feat a hero?

18. Who are some contemporary sports heroes? Is Kobe Bryant a hero? Why?

19. Who were some of the 20th century's sports heroes? Babe Ruth? Jesse Owens? Muhammad Ali? Michael Jordan? Pelé?

VOCABULARY

Working with your partner, try to define each of these words.

brave ....

virtuous ....

flaw ....

tragic ....

idol ....

idolized...

celebrity ....

tragedy ....

exception...

unsung hero ....

role model ....

heroic ....

NOTES & QUESTIONS

PROVERBS

Circle the two proverbs which you like the best.

Actions speak louder than words.

A hero is a man who is afraid to run away.—English

Heroism consists in hanging on one minute longer.—Norwegian

Death before dishonor.—Roman

Words are mere bubbles of water,
but deeds are drops of gold.—Chinese

The soldiers fight, and the kings are heroes.—Yiddish

THE CONVERSATION CONTINUES...

1. Who are some heroes of science or medicine?

2. Who are some heroes of aviation? Business?

3. Who are some people who are considered war heroes?

4. Were the fire fighters and police officers at the Twin Towers heroes? Why?

5. Who are some civil rights heroes? What did they do?

6. Can you think of some other political or historical heroes?

7. Whose faces are on American coins? Why is each person considered an American hero?

8. Who are some people on American dollar bills? Why are they considered heroes?

9. Why do you think Abraham Lincoln is considered a tragic hero?

10. What are some of the dangers of being a hero? Are there disadvantages to having heroes?

11. How can heroes inspire us? What are some heroic qualities?

12. Can you think of somebody who was once considered a hero and then lost his status?

13. What is an unsung hero? Have you ever personally known an unsung hero? Who? Why do you regard that person as a hero?

14. Did you ever regard anyone in your family as a hero? Why? How old were you?

15. Have you ever looked up to a friend as a hero? Do you still feel that way? Why?

16. Do you have a personal hero? Who? Why?

QUOTATIONS

Read all the quotations. Then, select your favorite and explain it to your class partner.

1. "One cannot always be a hero, but one can always be a human."
   —Johann Wolfgang von Goethe (1749–1832), German playwright and novelist

2. "You must do things you think you cannot do."
   —Eleanor Roosevelt (1884–1962), former First Lady, diplomat

3. "Self-trust is the essence of heroism."
   —Ralph Waldo Emerson (1803–1882), philosopher

4. "Who is a hero? He who conquers his urges."—The Talmud

5. "No sadder proof can be given by a man of his own littleness than disbelief in great men."
   —Thomas Carlyle (1795–1881), British historian

6. "Cowards die many times before their deaths; The valiant never taste of death but once."
   —William Shakespeare (1564–1616), English playwright

7. "Every owner is a Napoleon to their dog, hence the popularity of dogs."—Aldous Huxley (1894–1963), British novelist

8. "We can't all be heroes because somebody has to sit on the curb and clap as they go by."—Will Rogers (1879–1935), American humorist

9. "In me, it's caution. In someone else, it's cowardice."
   —Henny Youngman (1906–1998), American comedian

10. "My life is my message."
    —Mahatma Gandhi (1869–1948), Leader of India

11. "Show me a hero, and I'll write you a tragedy."
    —F. Scott Fitzgerald (1896–1940), writer

12. "How important it is for us to recognize and celebrate our heroes and she-ores!"
    —Maya Angelou (1928–), American poet

13. " Those who say that we're in a time when there are no heroes just don't know where to look."
    —Ronald Reagan (1911–2004), 40th U.S. President

14. "A hero is an ordinary individual who finds the strength to preserve and endure in spite of overwhelming obstacles."
    —Christopher Reeve (1952–2004), American actor

ON YOUR OWN

If you were a Superhero, what power would you want the most? To fly? To see through walls? Super strength like The Hulk?

Write a short paragraph explaining why you chose that power and read it to the class.

"All's well that ends well."

WILLIAM SHAKESPEARE
(1564–1616), playwright and poet

Appendix

TIPS & GENTLE ADVICE FOR ESL/EFL TEACHERS

ESL conversation teachers stimulate conversation in English among their students, help students with English usage, and evaluate student participation, comprehension and pronunciation. These tasks are your main responsibilities. Students learn by doing, and your classroom provides a safe place for them to expand their verbal skills in English.

In order to accomplish these goals, you may use a variety of structures within a class period, depending upon the skill and comfort of your students in using *Compelling Conversations*. For example, you might introduce a lesson topic by discussing one or more of the quotations. Or, you might choose to introduce a topic by examining the vocabulary.

We've often found it helpful, especially in the beginning of the semester, for you to role play for the class a question/answer session with a student. At this time, you could demonstrate how to pass on a question if it makes one uncomfortable. Setting a time limit for the question/answer activity also helps and meets students' desires for structure. In general, each class should begin and end with the class as a single unit even if you have used small groups or conversation partners during the period to build greater class cohesion.

Also, many students stay more on task if they are required to report back to the class or hand in an assignment as a result of the small group or question/answer seg-

ment. While students are engaged in small groups or conversation, you may go from group to group to maintain their focus and encourage or evaluate participation, or you may use this time for one on one practice with individual students. In all these situations, you will be modeling appropriate, authentic conversation for your listeners.

Teachers can use the materials in *Compelling Conversations* in many ways. We've written no direction or suggestion in stone. We hope the materials stimulate interest and creativity in teachers as well in students.

Here are some suggestions for additional activities which have been successfully used in ESL classrooms:

- Start a lesson by selecting a question (e.g. What's your native country? How long did you live there?) and having each student tell his response to the class.

- Ask each student to tell the class a proverb from his country and explain it.

- Select a word with multiple purposes in English (e.g. play) and identify with them the differing definitions of the word. Students can write a sentence for each of the meanings.

- Select a common English word (e.g. play) and help students create a list of rhyming words (e.g. play, say, stay, day, bay etc.) and use the words in sentences.

- Identify a common prefix and help students create a list of words with this prefix.

- Identify a common suffix and help students create a list of words with this suffix.

- Have students create a word search using at least seven of the vocabulary words from a lesson. Students may then exchange these word searches with others in the class.

- Divide the class into groups of three or four and assign a quotation to each group. The group discusses the meaning of the quotation for 10 minutes and then a representative of the group reports back to the class as a whole.

- Pick two quotations with opposing points of view. With the help of students identify the meaning of each quote. Ask students their responses to each quote. Then take a class vote to determine which quotation seems most apt to students.

- Ask students to identify a situation in which they might use a proverb or quotation.

- Have students role play a situation in which they might use a proverb or quotation.

The possibilities remain endless. Build on your successes. Relax and have fun. Remember, the greatest motivators in your classroom remain your encouragement, enthusiasm, and example.

BIBLIOGRAPHY

21st Century Dictionary of Quotations. Dell Publishing, 1993.

Ackerman, Mary Alice. *Conversations on the Go.* Search Institute, 2004.

Akbar, Fatollah. *The Eye of an Ant: Persian Proverbs and Poems.* Iranbooks, 1995.

Ben Shea, Noah. *Great Jewish Quotes: Five Thousand Years of Truth and Humor from the Bible to George Burns.* Ballantine Books, 1993.

Berman, Louis A. *Proverb Wit and Wisdom: A Treasury of Proverbs, Parodies, Quips, Quotes, Cliches, Catchwords, Epigrams, and Aphorisms.* Perigee Book, 1997.

Bierce, Ambrose. *The Devil's Dictionary.* Dover Publications, 1993.

Bullivant, Alison. *The Little Book of Humorous Quotations.* Barnes & Noble Books, 2002.

Byrne, Robert. *1,911 Best Things Anybody Ever Said.* Ballantine Books, 1988.

Cohen, M. J. *The Penguin Dictionary of Epigrams.* Penguin, 2001.

Esar, Evan. *20,000 Quips and Quotes.* Barnes & Noble Books. 1995.

Frank, Leonard Roy. *Freedom: Quotes and Passages from the World's Greatest Freethinkers.* Random House, 2003.

Galef, David. *Even Monkeys Fall From Trees: The Wit and Wisdom of Japanese Proverbs.* Tuttle Publishing, 1987.

Galef, David. *Even a Stone Buddha Can Talk: More Wit and Wisdom of Japanese Proverbs.* Tuttle Publishing, 2000.

Gross, David C. and Gross, Esther R.. *Jewish Wisdom: A Treasury of Proverbs, Maxims, Aphorisms, Wise Sayings, and Memorable Quotations.* Walker and Company, 1992.

Gross, John. *The Oxford Book of Aphorisms.* Oxford University Press, 1987.

Habibian, Simin K. *1001 Persian-English Proverbs: Learning Language and Culture Through Commonly Used Sayings.* Third Edition. Ibex Publishers, 2002.

Jacobs, Ben and Hjalmarsson, Helena. *The Quotable Book Lover.* Barnes & Noble, 2002.

Jarski, Rosemarie. *Wisecracks: Great Lines from the Classic Hollywood Era.* Contemporary Books, 1999.

Lewis, Edward and Myers, Robert. *A Treasury of Mark Twain: The Greatest Humor of the Greatest American Humorist.* Hallmark Cards, 1967.

McLellan, Vern. *Quips, Quotes, and Quests.* Harvest Books, 1982.

MacHale, Des. *Wit.* Andrews McMeel Publishing, 2003.

McWilliams, Peter. *Life 101: Everything We Wish We Had Learned About Life In School – But Didn't.* Prelude Press, 1991.

The Oxford Dictionary of Quotations, 5th Edition.. Oxford University Press, 1999.

Peter, Dr. Laurence J. *Peter's Quotations: Ideas for Our Time.* William Morrow, 1977.

Pickney, Maggie. *Pocket Positives For Our Times.* The Five Mile Press, 2002.

Pickney, Maggie. *The Devil's Collection: A Cynic's Dictionary.* The Five Mile Press, 2003.

Platt, Suzy. *Respectfully Quoted: A Dictionary of Quotations.* Barnes & Noble Books, 1993.

Poole, Garry. *The Complete Book of Questions.* Willow-Creek Association, 2003.

Rado, Adam. *Conversation Pieces.* Aethron Press. 2001.

Reader's Digest Quotable Quotes: Wit and Wisdom for All Occasions From America's Most Popular Magazine. Reader's Digest, 1997

Rosten, Leo. *Rome Wasn't Burned in a Day; The Mischief of Language.* Doubleday, 1972.

Rosten, Leo. *Leo Rosten's Carnival of Wit.* Penguin Books USA, 1994.

Shalit, Gene. *Great Hollywood Wit: A Glorious Cavalcade of Hollywood Wisecracks, Zingers, Japes, Quips, Slings, Jests, Snappers, and Sass from the Stars.* St. Martin's Griffin, 2002

Simpson, James Beasley. *Best Quotes of '54, '55, '56.* Thomas Y. Crowell Company, 1957.

Stavropoulos, Steven. *The Wisdom of the Ancient Greeks: Timeless Advice on the Senses, Society, and the Soul.* Barnes & Noble Books, 2003.

Sullivan, George. *Quotable Hollywood.* Barnes and Noble, 2001.

Webster's Dictionary of Quotations. Merriam-Webster, 1992.

Williams, Rose. *Latin Quips at Your Fingertips: Witty Latin Sayings by Wise Romans.* Barnes and Noble, 2000.

Winokur, Jon. *The Portable Curmudgeon.* Jon. New American Library, 1987.

Winkour, Jon. *Zen to Go.* New American Library, 1989.

Winkour, Jon. *The Traveling Curmudgeon.* Sasquatch Books, 2003.

Yong-chol, Kim. *Proverbs East and West: An Anthology of Chinese, Korean, and Japanese Saying with Western Equivalents.* Hollym, 1991.

Zubko, Andy. *Treasury of Spiritual Wisdom: A Collection of 10,000 Inspirational Quotations.* Blue Dove Press. 1996.

The internet has dramatically expanded our access to quotations. Five websites deserve to be mentioned here as outstanding sources.
• www.bartleby.com/quotations
• www.qotd.org
• www.quotationspage.com
• www.thinkexist.com
• http://en.wikiquote.org

ABOUT THE AUTHORS

ERIC H. ROTH

Born in New York City and raised in Indiana, Eric Roth has taught English and writing in California for the last dozen years.

Roth currently teaches undergraduate engineering students and graduate science students the pleasures of writing and public speaking in English at the University of Southern California.

A freelance writer and former Congressional aide, he has also taught numerous courses at Santa Monica College, UCLA Extension, and Cal State, Long Beach's American Language Institute.

In 1995, Roth taught the first citizenship class in the Santa Monica-Malibu Unified School District and served as the first director of the Community Enhancement Services Adult Education Center in 1996. Several hundred graduates of these courses passed their citizenship exams and became naturalized American citizens.

Roth received his M.A. in Media Studies in 1988 from the New School for Social Research. He is a member of numerous professional organizations, including the International Communication Association, Teaching English to Speakers of Other Languages, and California Association of Teaching English to Speakers of Other Languages. Roth has given several teacher workshops.

As you might guess, he enjoys talking with friends, relatives, students and fellow teachers.

TONI ABERSON

After 35 years of teaching English and supervising English teachers, Toni Aberson (M.A. English; M.A. Psychology and Religion) believes that a lively classroom is the optimal learning environment.

"If people are thinking, sharing, and laughing, then they're learning," notes Aberson. "The mere fact that those adults are in an ESL classroom attests to their courage and their determination to learn."

"Adult ESL students bring a wealth of interesting experiences with them," continues Aberson. "They bring the world into the classroom. The challenge for ESL teachers is to put students at ease and encourage them to practice English. What better way than to ask students about their lives? I love teaching ESL."

P.S. Eric Roth calls Toni "mom."

ONLINE

Compelling Conversations is the first book by Aberson or Roth. Visit www.compellingconversations.com to offer feedback, suggest conversation topics, or contribute questions, proverbs, or quotations.